D0800730

UNLIMITED
LEARNINGS

UNLIMITED LEARNINGS

(Because Life Never Stops Teaching)

with emphasis
on
Compassion, Gratitude,
Positivity and Mindfulness.

DEEPAK CHOPRA

PARTRIDGE

Copyright © 2017 by DEEPAK CHOPRA.

ISBN: Softcover   978-1-5437-0032-9
               eBook   978-1-5437-0031-2

All rights reserved. No part of this book may be used or reproduced
by any means, graphic, electronic, or mechanical, including
photocopying, recording, taping or by any information storage
retrieval system without the written permission of the author except
in the case of brief quotations embodied in critical articles and
reviews.

Because of the dynamic nature of the Internet, any web addresses
or links contained in this book may have changed since publication
and may no longer be valid. The views expressed in this work are
solely those of the author and do not necessarily reflect the views of
the publisher, and the publisher hereby disclaims any responsibility
for them.

Print information available on the last page.

To order additional copies of this book, contact
Partridge India
000 800 10062 62
orders.india@partridgepublishing.com

www.partridgepublishing.com/india

Sincerely dedicated with gratitude to all those
who gave me wonderful opportunities and helped me
face the challenges that Life offered,
&
to learn, develop and grow into
the individual I am today.
Finally, with love to my grand children
Nabhya, Aysha and Khush
while sincerely wishing that

Unlimited Learnings

guides and helps the future generations
in their endeavours
to become better & compassionate human beings
such that their life journey becomes
wonderfully satisfying,
one full of
gratitude, compassion and positivity.

Happy moments, praise God.

Difficult times, seek God.

Quiet moments, worship God.

Painful moments, trust God.

Every moment, thank God.

Preface

I had concluded in my 1st book - "*Life's Little Learnings*" (published in Sept'2015) - under the title "The view from here...........what next?" that:

During our difficult times, most of us are often unable to face the present, as also to look at our future optimistically. We instead think about it pessimistically. We normally forget that these tough times cannot last forever, and will pass soon. We also forget that we need to muster all our inner strengths to boldly face the current challenges, and look at the possibilities of a better tomorrow, instead of overly *concentrating* on today's problems.

We need to remember, that our ultimate success can come through only when we make a beginning somewhere, instead of waiting for it to *happen* on its own. We need to make a choice on that now. In fact, even the today that we are living is a collection of results of the choices we made in the past. In the same way, our today's decisions will be the base of our tomorrow's reality.

Our life ahead will be a culmination of various choices and decisions we make *today*, based on our experiences of yesterdays, and thereby opening up our tomorrows – the choice is all ours. Always...

Few important aspects from *Life's Little Learnings,* and may be also from our individual past and specific experiences, need to be relooked at, and then decide in favour of having a wonderful future & life ahead full of happiness, compassion and gratitude.

I had presented that book with hope, faith, belief, and confidence that its practical suggestions would help the readers get enough motivation to recognize their problems as challenges, and finally to tap inner resources to live their life well.

I dedicate this 2nd book also to all those who are engaged in and committed to make a difference through self-growth. I further hope that the readers get enough motivation to help themselves become a better person, acknowledge their abilities & capabilities, remain positive & grateful, and continue to attempt passing on this wonderful infection to their entire social environment.

I wish the readers good, happy and fulfilling times ahead in their respective lives.

Relax, and read this collection a little bit at a time, relate the learnings with your experiences and digest the contents as per your convenience, interest and growth.

There is no hurry to reach the end. Enjoy the journey! Enjoy your life!!

Spread happiness, positivity and compassion!!!
Live well!!!!
God bless all!!!!!

Deepak Chopra
Reach me at >> dchopra49@gmail.com

Acknowledgments

I offer my heartfelt thanks and gratitude to all those teachers, motivators, authors, columnists, spiritual leaders, and most importantly my social connections who have inspired me specifically during the last about 20 years of my life. I humbly extend my sincere acknowledgements to all of them. Every family member, friend, colleague, and casual acquaintance has made significant contribution in shaping my opinions and views besides teaching me invaluable lessons and moulding my personal life.

Life is a continuous series of lessons. Learning is truly a never-ending activity and by the grace of Almighty, I am happy to continue to learn today in the same way as in the past. I have gone through my share of turbulence, challenges and had my lows of life at various times. I faulted many times in personal relationships and would have hurt many. I, with the strength now gained through the new revelations and learnings, offer my earnest apologies to all those whom I might have hurt, and believe that I will be forgiven. In anticipation, I say a big "thank you" for all their benevolence and acceptance.

By the grace of Almighty, I have been able to develop discipline, sincerity, self-control and empathy which help me in facing challenges of my life, and am proud to continue practicing these significant values in my life.

I will always fall short of words to possibly express my special & heartfelt thanks to my loving wife Geeta - for all her sharing, understanding, support and encouragement. She deserves my countless "I love you".

I also owe my special thanks to my two grown up children for their love, and providing me with opportunities to understand my situations better, keeping in view the changing trends of the modern world, and finally enabling me to humbly change things which I could, and gracefully accept those which I couldn't. Love you, Deepta and Aloke.

By developing & practicing positive attitude, I can claim to be a much happier and confident person today to consciously spread compassion and positive vibrations around my family, friends & social environment.

I seek continued blessings and guidance of The Almighty on the path ahead in my life so that I can complete my life journey with as much gratitude and faith as possible.

I will be unjust to myself, if I start this book without repeating the SERENITY PRAYER which gives me the needed strength and encouragement every single time I say it:

> *God grant me:*
> *Serenity to accept the things that I can't change,*
> *Courage to change the things that I can, and*
> *Wisdom to know the difference between them.*

When you say the same, as many times as you think you need to and actually can, I am confident of its marvellous effect on your success too.

READER's COMMENTS ON LIFE's LITTLE LEARNINGS (author's 1st publication)

N Bhaskar, Hyderabad >>>

I have completed reading of – Life's Little Learnings. It is a good advice-bank useful for one's true life's journey with many cross roads, experiences of out-of-controls and outcomes from study of fellow human minds.

Suggestions to change out looks towards understanding problems arising from expectations of fast changing world can be well received by today's youth. Problem perspectives need more analysis, if the size of the book is not a restriction. It is a stack of synopses from references of social & behavioural sciences. Writings of Hanh, Freud, Maslow and other theories like X-Y theory of human nature, could have been scientifically narrated at appropriate places – Power of Breath, Relationships, Mirroring, Blame and responsibility- etc.

Good effort is seen in simplifying the presentation of problems, probable apt solutions, which otherwise, may go into volumes. The straight expressions of the author are well received.

And finally, it is a palm size counsellor to go into the pocket of every person, for primary knowledge about life, value of concern and power of love.

Preeti Manchanda, USA >>>

"Life's Little Learnings" is an easy to read book. With its short and crisp articles, one doesn't have to worry about reading it from beginning to end. I have kept it handy in my living and read it anytime I see it.

The simplified short article style of writing seems so new and fresh against the traditional Psychological books which go on to lengths to explain concepts and theories like a simple 'How to be Happy?'

For me, "Life's Little Learnings" is like a mini psychological encyclopaedia. Whenever I am feeling low or have questions about life, I open it randomly and surprisingly find my answers on the page which is opened automatically.

Can easily feel the spiritual bent of mind of the writer in his writings.

Rajesh Chugh, New Delhi >>>
I have read your book 'LIFE'S LITTLE LEARNINGS' with great interest. In fact, you have emphasized and focused on LIFE'S VITAL AND IMPORTANT LEARNINGS.

You are not only smart but wise as well, the book is written with great wisdom and experience.

S D Pandey, Kolkatta >>>
I read the book, "Life's Little Learnings" again before writing this brief review. It's a wonderful book which deals with our daily life. Chapters are well planned, duly illustrated with practical experiences from life, their pro & cons and solution to deal with them positively. Your style

of mixing dry subjects with interesting stories makes the reading absorbing.

To quote a few chapters, nails in the fence, fearful mouse, choices in life, hare and tortoise story retold, Mother Teresa's poem, stress free life, anger management and dealing with generation gap etc. make us to relook the way we lived and wasted a major part of our life to negativity. Any way, it's never too late to learn. With these lessons in mind we can make our remaining life positive & purposeful. We can mend bridges, revive lost relations and spread happiness.

The book is a 'Must read' for people of every age, particularly for young generation which is exposed to rising expectations, increasing competition and diminishing opportunities, leading stressful unhappy life. They need to learn that key to happiness is not in earning huge pay packets or accumulating material wealth. Happiness is a state of mind and it is easy to acquire. Similarly, they need to learn the difference between aspirations & expectations.

The book has come out very well. I wish the writer all the best.

Unlimited Learnings

<u>Contents</u>

Life's Little Learnings

Each of the following messages has proven & extra-ordinary transformative powers, holds an insight of wisdom to have happiness, and to live a wonderful life. As such, these are not merely *life-changers*, but can actually be *life-savers*.

- ❖ Live an authentic life: The commitment to live an authentic life i.e. to be true to ourselves, is a valuable gift we all can have. It may not be an easy task, since we will have to break free from the attractions or seductions of the environment, decide to live life on our own terms, and with our own values – duly aligned with our original dreams. Every decision we make and every step we take, must be an informed choice guided by our commitment to live a life that is true and honest to ourselves. For this, we have to identify and explore our deep-rooted hopes, desires, strengths and weaknesses. As we proceed on such a path, we can be certain to experience invaluable bliss and happiness - well beyond our highest imaginations!

- ❖ Live with kindness and forgiveness: It has been known from times immemorial, that our words are the *verbalised* form of our thoughts, and our deeds are the *actualised* form of our beliefs. How we treat someone else depends on how we treat ourselves: if we disrespect others, we disrespect ourselves; if we don't trust others, we are distrustful of ourselves; if we are cruel to others, we will be cruel to ourselves; if we don't appreciate those around us, we won't appreciate ourselves. Treating others and ourselves kindly is possible when we are willing to forgive others for all their faults and follies. And before that, we have to forgive ourselves! We all must make conscious efforts to be kinder than expected to every other person, and in everything we do. We must be more generous than anticipated, and more positive than we think is possible. Every moment spent with another human being should be treated as an opportunity to demonstrate our highest human values, and to influence him/ her with our humanity. We can thus make the whole world a better place to live in, may be one person at a time!

❖ <u>Live our dreams without fears</u>: What normally holds us back in life is the invisible framework of our fears, doubts and anxieties. Fear is an outcome of the thought of failure. Though it may help us remain in our comfort zones but in reality, the sense of fear increases the need to be extra cautious and vigilant. It further weakens the power of creativity of our mind besides reducing its flexibility. The greatest risk in life is taking no risks! Every time we are able to do something which had earlier created fear in our mind, we are able to get back that very power which fear had initially stolen from us. *Dar ke aagey jeet hai*!! Our strengths live on the other side of our fears.

Every time we step into the process of growth and progress – coming out of our safe and comfort zones – we can boldly face the daily challenges of our life. The more fears we can overcome, the more power we will be able to reclaim. This way, we will grow fearless and powerful, and thus be able to live the lives of our dreams!

Only those who will risk going too far can possibly find out how far one can go – T S Eliot.

❖ <u>Live a life full of love and happiness</u>: How well do we actually live depends on how much we love. And before loving anyone else, it is essential to learn to love ourselves. Our heart is wiser than our head. We need to honour it. Trust it. Follow it. We must celebrate all the simple pleasures available to us. None of this can happen overnight. But by working on it every day, we will live each day as if it was our whole life in a miniature form. The phenomenal power of love and its impact on ourselves, can be seen and understood by expressing it. We can build a beautiful life for ourselves and for those we love by being happy within us, and be willing to have fun. Then we can spread it as a *contagious* virus, to create a world of happy people!

❖ <u>Every big dream starts small</u>: The way we handle smallest things in our daily life perhaps is indicative of the way we do most of all other things. So, if we do our minor jobs well, we will also achieve excellence with our larger tasks. Every small or tiny effort builds on the next, so that magnificent things can be created – step by step. That takes our confidence to greater levels, and helps us realise our dreams. To solve a problem, there is no need to push ourselves too hard, because it might make things far worse, close down our mind, and actually prevent us from thinking creatively. To spot the new rising opportunities, which are always there in almost all situations, we just need to recognise and acknowledge them. We could be less fearful, less cautious, willing to remain open to new experiences, and happy to experiment. This will slowly and steadily open our minds, so as to focus on our lives in a pleasant manner. It is an established fact, that *small daily improvements* always lead to exceptional results over a period of time. A new confidence will then erupt, and enable us to face the challenges that come our way. *The tiniest of our actions is always better than the boldest of our intentions!!*

❖ <u>Choose our support systems carefully</u>: We all are social animals, and very much a part & parcel of our immediate environment consisting of things, places and people. We all move through our lives along with the people of our social world. And so, we must always be aware and careful of the things and the people we allow into our lives. It is a sure mark of wisdom, to choose to spend our time at those places & with those things that motivate & energise us, and to associate with those people who elevate & uplift us. We should avoid, all negative influences over our thoughts and general functioning, while welcoming every positive influence all the time. We should try, to find and maintain a positive attitude in negative situations. These most influential components of our support system will, directly inspire us to be our greatest selves - so as to lead our largest lives!

❖ Count our blessings: It is an irony that most of us do not realise what is more important in our life until we are too old to do anything about it. We spend many of our best years pursuing things that actually matter very little in the end. While our social world invites, coaxes and encourages us to fill our lives with material objects, we all know & can appreciate that the more basic pleasures are the ones that actually enrich and sustain us. Irrespective of how easy or hard our current conditions and situations are, we all have a wealth of simple blessings around us – just waiting to be counted. These blessings are our family, spouse, children, friends, food on our table, money in our bank, good health & digestion, and ability to see, hear, feel & think etc. And when we count our blessings, our happiness grows, our gratitude expands and each day becomes a breath-taking gift of our life!

❖ Practice Mindfulness: Mindfulness is all about being compassionate, observing without criticism, and living in the moment. When unhappiness or stress occurs, we need to learn to treat them as if they were some black clouds in the sky which will disappear – in the same manner as they initially appeared. We need to appreciate that our unhappiness, stress, anxiety and tension are not "problems" that can be solved. Actually, they are *emotions* and as such can only be *felt!* We have to learn to see the situation, the environment, and our emotional difficulties from a different place and in a different light – by changing our perspective. This will transform our experiences of life. Mindfulness allows us to catch negative thought patterns before they move us on a downward spiral. It allows us to deal with our imagined problems in the most effective way possible, and at the most appropriate moment. Mindfulness finally allows us to experience the world calmly, non-judgmentally and encourages us to treat ourselves and all others with compassion. That liberates us from pain and worry and arouses a true sense of happiness that will spill into our daily lives. It brings in greater clarity for us to take wiser and more considered decisions, to change things which can be changed, and accept those which cannot be changed. Remember the *Serenity Prayer*!

❖ Be of use to others & make a difference: We get a chance to express our personal talents through the work done by us, so that we can *create* our own life and realise our true potential. We should therefore work with devotion, passion, energy and have an eye for excellence. By adopting such a dedicated way of life, our productivity will not only become a source of inspiration, it will also impact other people by making a difference in their lives. One of the greatest secrets to a beautiful life is to *do such work that matters*. For ourselves as well as all others! Our work thus becomes a suitable source for discovering more of our inner-gifts, displaying more of our potential, and giving us more confidence. We can become successful, on our own terms rather than those dictated by our environment. But for all this, we need to make significant changes to make our own life matter. We should attempt to be of as much use and service to as many people as possible. This is how each one of us can shift from the realm of the ordinary into the heights of the extraordinary. Sometimes, our contributions may not be substantial, but it is important that we *do contribute*. We need to work upon leaving a legacy: not about making money or receiving appreciation but about leaving an influence and impact on our fellow beings, besides making this world a better place to live for our next generations!

What we all need to do is to look ahead five years from now, and try to predict what things of our current life we will regret the most. Then, we should take appropriate actions *today* to avoid or prevent those regrets at a *later* date. No one can move forward while looking back! And there is nothing we can do to change the past!! We can at best attempt, and be determined to handle our present in a manner that our future is what we would ideally want it to be.

It is not difficult to appreciate that *now* is the future that we promised ourselves last year or last month or last week. This *now* is the only moment that we really have.

As I stated at the start, these simple and little learnings do have the power of becoming *life-changers* or perhaps *life-savers* for our own selves, as well as for all others in our life!! I can safely vouch that "I can, I will and I believe" has the power!!

THE POWER OF ONE

In today's complex and fast-paced world, it is quite common to find ourselves feeling overwhelmed, confused, in a state of dissatisfaction and powerless. We feel that our social problems are inflexible; political situations seem hopeless; financial stress is widespread; and we are unable to contribute anything positive or constructive to improve the situation.

These factors multiply our problems. Sometimes, it even feels like beyond our capacity to handle and we ask: "What can I do? I am just one person! I am alone!!".

To overcome such feelings of powerlessness and hopelessness, we need to keep in mind the basic fact - which we already know but usually forget – that:

> One person can make a difference. One action can transform a relationship.
>
> One word can change a conversation. One tree can start a forest.
>
> One smile can begin a friendship. One touch can show you care.
>
> One sunbeam can light a room. One candle can wipe out darkness.

One hope can raise our spirits. One person can change our life.

That difference starts with ourselves!

Such is the Power of One that it can turn our attitude around – in fact turn our life around - one page at a time, one story at a time, one word at a time, one step at a time!!

<u>Objective of Life</u>

Life goes on, for ever. And life can be as easy or difficult as we make it. It is actually the sum total of our thoughts and beliefs about it. Well, it is also to be understood that our life need not always be a struggle. When we struggle, and push too hard, it creates resistance and that opposition unnecessarily makes life more difficult.

Apart from death, there are only two things absolutely certain – <u>*change*</u> and <u>*uncertainty*</u>. If we can learn to be happy with both, we can master our fate and destiny, in order to have "lived a life". Over the duration ahead in our life, we need to learn: to be stronger, able to build a vast inner capacity of positive energy & personal power, continue cultivating self-esteem, self-confidence, and self-belief.

We need to understand, that self-belief is our secret partner which we can turn "on" when we need it most. Our greatest battle is always with *ourselves* - since our most powerful enemy is within us only. And so is our self-belief. Our mind is our weapon, and our mental attitude makes us strong or weak. Our biggest challenge is to conquer ourselves. Our unlimited power house of self-belief needs to be always kept in mind, to change some aspects of our life, attitude and behaviour.

We need to start *loving* and *believing in* ourselves. Just a simple decision is required to appreciate ourselves more, give credit where it is due, and cultivate compassion, respect, well-defined principles, ethics and value system for ourselves.

It is recommended to develop generosity, openness and tolerance replacing criticism, meanness and bitterness. To convert these *concepts* into practice, we need to *do* acts commensurate with their inherent characteristics – being generous, doing acts of kindness, and accepting others as they are etc.

It is always important to know where we are going instead of knowing where we are coming from.

Being true to ourselves is the real truth. We should stop looking for outside respect, admiration and approval. Let us learn to generate our own feel-good factors to grow into a mature, wise and developed person. At the same time, our motivation needs to be of the highest order to pull through the difficult phases of life, and to meet our challenges head-on.

To really understand as to what matters to us the most, and to maintain our life in this context, here is a simple exercise:

Answer these questions in maximum of 10 words:

- What do I want most out of my life?
- What do I want to see happening in the world?
- What qualities or virtues make me special?
- What things I am capable of, or can do at this time?

Now, frame this statement which will become our true objective of life:

I will .... (select one answer from q4.), using my .... (answer from q3), to accomplish .... (answer from q2), and in so doing achieve .... (answer from q1).

Try this out and see if it makes sense.

Revered Dalai Lama has said that "our outlook and state of mind is important to determine our level of happiness – irrespective of the environmental conditions. And, our outlook can be modified by deliberately developing inner compassion and serenity that is not affected by changes in circumstances. The greater is the calmness of our mind, the greater will be our peace of mind and our ability to enjoy a happy & blissful life".

For this he has recommended two methods: one is to learn to appreciate and be content with what we already have; and second is to increase our self-worth and dignity.

Gratitude & Positive Reinforcement

The fact and realisation that we have lived to see another day, should make us feel grateful, towards all the forces of nature. We also need to express gratitude to our fellow beings, for being generous and helpful in making our journey-so-far joyous and purposeful. Gratitude turns what we have into enough, and more. It turns denial into acceptance, chaos into order, and confusion into clarity. It makes sense of the past, brings peace for today and creates a vision for tomorrow. It further makes us calmer and serene. Expressing gratitude makes us happier and richer in our emotional contentment, and feelings of love & compassion, besides exhibiting the other positive qualities of our head and heart.

Positive reinforcement (+R) and constructive feedback from those around us…our family, co-workers and people in our social circle…is the thing we need the most, and strangely we often receive it the least. In fact, we can use positive reinforcement for sustainable behaviour change in ourselves, as also in those we interact with every day. It could be one of the most powerful forces on the planet for improving overall performance.

Today even business houses share a common dream: to improve business performance, increase profits, and are always in search of better results. It needs to be understood that to change results, the behaviour of people has to change. The usual changes are expected in the areas of efficiency, integrity, dependability, honesty, courage, decisiveness etc. While all these are important, there is one quality that everyone normally overlooks – the ability to change our own, as also the behaviour of others around us, to improve overall performance of any setup.

Since performance improvement is every individual's greatest challenge and opportunity, the art of +R behaviour change is something every one of us should master.

We all instinctively know that we feel good when we are offered sincere, specific and positive feedback. Then why are fewer and fewer people using it? What can and should be done to assure its presence and availability to realise and see the positive impact it will make on the status of our lives?

Stop Regretting - Take Action Fearlessly

"Our biggest regrets are not for the things we have done, but for the things we haven't done" – Chad Michael Murray.

It is a well-known fact, though not commonly understood or appreciated, that regretting is a complete waste of time besides being a very negative feeling. Regretting, for sure does not change anything at all, and no one has ever been able to improve anything with just regret. If we want to improve our life and move forwards to a better future, we need to stop regretting. NOW! We need to start looking at what we have now that is good for us, and how/ what to add to it and make everything even better. We need to remember that everything in this life brings something positive. The real test is to find that positive.

Each of us makes mistakes – we all have, and would continue to. Without mistakes, no one can succeed. Let us not blame ourselves for making a particular choice at the specific moment. Given the wisdom and strength, and under certain circumstances, we make certain choices and if those happen not to be completely right or correct, so it be. Yes, we will have some regrets, but we also have the choice to focus on the benefits those choices and decisions have brought. The worst is, to let ourselves be controlled by our feelings of continuous regret. Our choices shape us as a person, and our experience make us the person we are.

When we accept that regret is a total waste of time, we need to change things we are used to do in a routine manner, besides thinking differently about our world. Asking ourselves questions is one of the best ways to change our life. It begins with changing our thinking, and then our actions need to follow.

So, the question to ask ourselves is: "If I continue doing what I am doing every day, where will I be in five years from now? Will my life be any different?"

To make any difference, it is important to first decide what we want that will take us towards improving our life. Then ask ourselves "what can I do today as my first small step?" Often the most difficult thing is getting started – and once we are able to do so we will feel better, and moving on our chosen path. We must first know what we want to change, and believe that we can decide in doing it.

> *"Never look back unless you are planning to go that way"* – Henry David Thoreau.

Before we try to change our life, we need to look at our attitude. We need to believe that we deserve better, and then it becomes possible to cross our stumbling blocks.

The biggest obstacle to our taking any action is fear – fear of failure, loss, embarrassment, criticism or even ridicule. To achieve all that is possible for us, we must consciously and deliberately take control of our fears that hold us back.

Our self-confidence is the antidote to our fears. It gives us the energy, enthusiasm and necessary drive to overcome our obstacles in order to reach our goals. It is based on a foundation of courage, and courage is the key to success.

It is true that everyone is afraid of some things, and many times of many things. The prime difference is how we deal with the normal and natural fears that we experience each day, or how easily we succumb to them. It has been proven scientifically that to overcome our fears and develop courage & self-confidence, we should do the very thing we fear, times and again, until the fear is gone.

As we move toward the situation that we fear and take some action in spite of our fear, the fear goes away and its place is taken by courage. However, if we back away from that situation, the fear grows and consumes our thoughts and feelings which in turn distract and disturb us the whole day.

One of the greatest fear that normally holds back any person from an action is the fear of rejection. The concern as to what other people may think about us often holds us back from trying in the very first place.

Many people stay in unhappy relationship, bad marriage, bad job or a difficult situation because they are always so concerned that others will be critical of them, if they decide to get out of that situation. And, when they do muster up all the courage to walk away, they are quite often surprised that no one was really bothered about it, or cared. It was simply their own thoughts and unfounded fears.

There is always a choice – to act or not to act - and decision is ours.

> *"Life isn't about finding yourself. It is about creating yourself"* - George Bernard Shaw

Our Thoughts, Words and Actions

Blame, resentment and bitterness have serious consequences, and start a chain reaction in our life. It is such a common thing, and quite unusual to find someone who is not blaming his/ her parents/ partner or circumstances for something or the other. Such thoughts do not allow us to have a <u>terrific</u> life, but instead create a <u>terrible</u> life. They make us powerless.

Powerless people moan and victims whine. In contrast, powerful people are happy and have a distinct aura around them. An attitude of gratitude takes us from being a victim to becoming victorious. Studies confirm that people who express gratitude increase their happiness levels, lower their blood pressure levels, get better quality sleep, improve their relationships, experience a positive impact on their depressive moods and are less affected by pain.

To take responsibility for creating our life, we will need to challenge all kinds of blames, excuses and look deeply at our attitude. This will make us feel lighter, and free enough to be non-judgmental about others or circumstances. We will be able to <u>not carry</u> around baggage from our past, or accumulate it in our present life.

Seeing ourselves as a driving force in our life is a choice! Choices have to be made, come what may. We need to choose our choices!! To be happy, is yet another important choice and decision. We can train our mind, body and emotions to link our pains or pleasures to whatever we choose, and to create the life that we want. We are the masters of our thoughts and we need to believe in our own potential.

Once such choices have been made, we can work upon increasing our confidence, motivation, and inspiration to become more powerful – to dictate and *change* our own life. Any change can only be brought about by our own actions and none else can do it for us. Mere thinking "if I had more confidence, then I would get things done" does not bring in the desired results. Decisions have to be taken to act, and there is no substitute for action.

And for some reasons, if our action is not bringing results, we need to draw back and examine our methods - there must be a better way of achieving our objective? We need to adapt, and change directions. When action is focussed and appropriate, only then it serves us in getting the right results. We should remember that there is no such thing as failure – there are only actions and consequences. It is our own interpretation, through which we label things as success or failure.

"If we keep on doing things the same way, we will get the same results" is a famous saying.

Also, *"it is not because things are difficult that we do not dare; it is because we do not dare that things are difficult"*.

Swami Vivekananda has said: *"The calmer we are, the less disturbed our nerves will be, the more shall we love, and the better will our work be"*.

Getting into the right frame of mind is therefore of key importance. Any negative thought in our mind, has a direct effect on our immune system and cell functioning. Our thoughts, feelings and attitudes influence what we attract into our lives, and we are responsible for the results thereof.

We can all bring in a little magic in our lives, by changing our *thoughts & mind* about anything that is not to our liking. This will help us demonstrate, and live through our new thoughts, and then move towards that new reality.

We should remember that we are answerable to ourselves for our every thought, action and decision. This will increase our personal integrity, so as to recommit and reaffirm ourselves, in the eventuality of straying away from our path and goals.

Our thoughts, words and actions are our critical tools, to manifest our desired destiny. (Readers are requested to refer to this, also under "Controlling our mind").

A Smile

A smile is defined as a simple curvature of the lips. It is a facial expression characterised by an upward curving of the corners of the mouth and indicating kindness, warmth, and pleasure. It is a noun and a verb at the same time, and an important, powerful and free tool available to us for communication.

A smile crosses languages, international borders and is a unique facial beautifier. It affects our mood, attitude and appearance in dramatic ways. A genuine smile has the power to change a pre-conceived opinion, or even break the tension in an uncomfortable situation. It is not only our lips that smile, our eyes smile as well. We can see this demonstrated by looking at the mirror while smiling, and hiding our face below the eyes. Through smile, kindness travels to our eyes, heart and soul. And kindness is a language which the deaf can hear and the blind can see!

Still, many people are afraid to smile, thinking that they will become vulnerable and may make them more approachable, while they may want to remain distant. Some others feel that smiling eliminates the invisible wall created by themselves between them and the world. The true meaning behind a smile may be difficult to detect and may even be misleading some times. But a genuine smile can actually turn someone's day around!

A smile is always quite contagious, and produces an immediate, automatic and natural reaction. Contagious here is the positive complimentary characteristic, and not in the negative sense as this word is generally understood. When we smile, it shows that we are happy and it is an established – though strange – fact that a simple smile itself can make us happy.

This world would be a much nicer place to live if we all displayed a sincere, genuine smile & attitude, and continue to infect everyone else we meet with a *contagious* smile and a positive *communicable* attitude.

We can all practice to smile more, and cherish the positive effect it will have on ourselves and the people in our world.

Our Needs and Wants: effects on our inner peace

Life, in general, has not changed over the years; it is only the surroundings and circumstances that have changed. The way we choose to react to those changes, determines the direct effect on the quality of our life. We need to focus on the need of distinguishing, between the ever-increasing responsibilities on our shoulders and other insignificant matters that consume our precious time.

Our needs and wants are two distinct entities. We need to separate our *needs* from our *wants* in order to achieve satisfaction. It is definitely not a simple matter. The dilemma is that we all <u>want</u> everything, but we don't <u>need</u> everything we want. When we can *quiet the unnecessary*, we can give an opportunity to *hear the necessary*. We need to edit our to-do-lists to handle the important tasks at hand, and avoid unnecessary burdens of other unimportant matters that we carry out.

When our mind is filled with petty things in life, there is no room for peace to enter. Try to compare this dilemma by knowing the capacity of our computer's hard drive, and what all can be stored or downloaded onto it. It contains unused programs, useless downloads that have nothing positive or valuable, but they take up major space. For a human mind, such useless things could be our unnecessary worries, anxieties, pressures and the unnecessary importance we place on unimportant matters or petty things.

Inner peace and outer peace are intertwined, and if inner peace is truly to be attained, we will have to work from the inside out. To have peace does not mean, to be in a place where there is no noise or trouble. It simply means to be in the midst of those things, and still be calm - deep within our heart.

In order to get rid of our disturbances and to attain peace, we need to develop and master the ability to be tolerant. We all know our personal limitations quite well. So, we need to learn the art of tolerance, as how to push beyond those limits before giving our response to situations. Tolerance is patience, and belief that we don't always have to be right. It is acceptance of other's view points and beliefs as well.

Our maturity and wisdom teaches us to make life less complicated by learning to agree to disagree.

Everything Big Starts with Something Little

There is great power in taking small steps. Many people are not moving forward today, simply because they are not willing to take those small steps. If we have a dream to go into any particular area, we should leap at the opportunity – no matter how small – to move in the direction of our dreams.

For example: if we dream of being a college sports coach but keep sitting at home waiting for an invitation from some college, we should know that the call may never come. We need to find an opportunity to coach somewhere, in fact anywhere. Find a young person, a young team, jump in and impart training, like we would if we were coaching at the highest level. Such initiative and experience, will give us sufficient boost to reach our goals, and actually become a sport coach one day.

We should not be afraid to take small steps. There's something powerful about momentum...no matter how little. Many times, the impossible is simply the untried. When we are immobilised with fear, when each task ahead appears to be a huge one, when we are unable to lift ourselves to face it – at those moments we can break the dilemma by using two simple words: "Do something!" By taking some small steps, the required momentum will begin to come into our life.

Most people don't succeed because they are too afraid to even try. As incredible as it sounds, they decide in advance that they are going to fail. Many times, our final goal seems so distant & unachievable that we don't even make an effort. But, once we have made our decision and actually start, it's like we are halfway there.

As we climb higher on any difficult mountain, we are able to see much farther. Same way, let us not be afraid at the beginning itself. Little achievements add up, and they add up rapidly. We need not worry only about our long-term goals in the beginning itself, and at least take the steps which move us past the starting point. Soon we will get to a point of no return, and moving towards our goals. We got to start - no matter what the circumstances – and take that first step! It is that simple.

We got to learn how to set deadlines, deal with negative feedback, be open to change, control our fear & worry, and succeed. We should not wait one extra moment, to begin our becoming the person we are meant and desire to be.

<u>Unchaining our elephant</u>

When an elephant baby is born into captivity, the owner ties the infant to a tree or a post with a thick chain in order to prevent it from escaping. During the first few weeks, the baby elephant tries to break the chain in an attempt to free himself from the chain and wander as his nature urges him to do. But, the strength of the steel chain is too huge against his childish efforts.

Over the next few weeks, he learns that his resources are far too less against the hardness of the chain. He gives up any further attempts and relegates himself to a life within a small circle.

As an adult elephant, conditioned by past experience, he can be even tied up to a small tree with the thinnest of ropes or, in some cases, no rope at all. He makes no attempts to wander because he carries with him, for the rest of his life, the belief that he does not possess the power to break the ties that bind him.

The adult elephant could easily snap the rope or uproot the tree to which it is attached, but he makes no such effort, because early in life, he was taught that true freedom was not available to him. For the rest of his life, he is tame and nothing like the captivating, powerful creature he was born to be.

Should we sympathise with this elephant?

Do we also, at times, feel that our life has been restricted by what we were conditioned to believe when we were very young? Maybe the conditioning was even more recent than that.

We all have doubts, fears and disappointments in our life. The challenge is to get out of our own way, face our self-limiting beliefs, and embrace our hidden creativity.

It's a blueprint to unleash our full potential!

It's time to unchain our elephant!!

<u>Understanding Insecurities</u>

The hard reality of life is that we all are suffering from insecurity to some extent.

Insecurity is defined as a fear of not being good enough, feeling that we do not match up to others expectations of us, or that we do not deserve to have the same things as others. We all can sometimes feel like this in some area of our lives. It is simply because when we don't feel secure, we feel insecure.

Insecurity is the feeling of not being sure about a certain outcome. It is usually associated with the future. For example, a person may be feeling insecure about a future aspect of his life or he may be afraid to lose something in the future that he already owns presently. Insecurity comes in various shapes and forms in our lives, and causes negative feelings to overshadow our true worth. When we have loads of insecure feelings, it robs us of the chance to realise our full potential, and that in turn results in enjoying less of life.

Some examples - an extrovert person may be using this behaviour to hide some deep-down insecurities; another person behaving with arrogance may be covering for his feelings of inferiority complex; a normal person could be having depressive thoughts such as "I _will never_ achieve anything", "I _can never_ have happy relationships", and "I am fat, ugly or unattractive" etc. These feelings which arise from our false belief that we are not good enough, can rob us of our dreams, and stop us from living the life we want to live.

Here are some more examples of situations where we may feel insecure:

a. feeling insecure about our job or finances: we may be afraid to lose our current job, or be afraid to be laid off in an expected downsizing plan of the company where we work. One of the things, that can help us eliminate this feeling completely is to have another source of income, or a backup plan including acquiring required skills for another job.

b. feeling insecure about a relationship: and always be thinking of the day this relationship might end. Here, we must build self-confidence and improve our self-image.

c. feeling that we might be losing on our critical support system − e.g. death of a dear one - on whom we have been solely dependent during other times of our crisis situation(s) in the past.

There are many other reasons like these, that can make us feel insecure. These are primarily, a result of not being sure of our abilities or of our job skills.

Another major reason that can cause insecurity is, having been raised in an environment that itself was full of uncertainty and insecurity. For example, most children who are brought up in families having financial problems or families that are constantly worried about money matters turn out to be financially insecure adults.

When we ignore, and allow our insecurity problems to accumulate, it can also bring in depression, because when important issues are ignored and no action is taken to resolve them at the appropriate moment, depression sets in. Some people face depressive moments as soon as they encounter them, while others bury them deeply in their mind, or throw them behind their backs. As a result, their subconscious mind usually responds back with depression at a later stage. We should therefore, deal with our problems right away, instead of ignoring them.

In order to deal with our feelings of insecurity, we must identify and fight the root cause, which in the first place, started the feelings of insecurity. Then we should look at developing those abilities and strengths, which will make us feel secure and confident. This itself will be a good step, and help us start the process of eliminating feelings of insecurity.

How to Overcome Insecurities

To overcome insecurity, we therefore need to change the way we feel about ourselves, and build on our security & confidence factors.

As an exercise, one way of doing this is to start a daily journal, and write down our feelings and behaviour. There will be some particular behaviour, which is obvious from our inner feelings of insecurity. So, we need to watch for it, and also examine what beliefs we are holding that make us feel insecure: are these rational beliefs?

Having done this, we need to examine what change in our behaviour is required to overcome our feelings of insecurity. We can also write down the benefits of overcoming these insecurities, and what have we missed out so far as a result of those insecurities. Then make a plan of how we are going to behave from now on. Write down the problems we anticipate. Accept that it won't be easy – since there will be times when we will find ourselves slipping back into our old ways - but at least we will be aware of it when this is happening.

Another way to overcome our insecurities is through simple affirmations, which are always of great help. Try repeating statements such as "I like myself", "I can do this", "I will do this", "I believe in myself" etc. Every morning when we look in the mirror, let us give ourselves a big smile and start liking the person we see reflected back at us by saying "I love you".

Taking proper care of ourselves - by making sure we eat a healthy & nutritious diet - and to do regular exercise is another very helpful tool. Nothing stops us to undergo regular facials, manicures, pedicures and massages – and pamper ourselves occasionally. This will signal to our subconscious mind that we are definitely worthy of taking care of ourselves. We can also plan other special treats into our normal day, such as coffee, movie, outing, some entertainment and gossip with friends or just time for ourselves to work on an activity we enjoy.

If our insecurity is the result of a past hurt, we can try talking it through with a trusted friend or family member. We can even write a <u>dummy</u> letter to the person who hurt us, expressing our hurt feelings: we don't have to actually send this letter; just the act of writing down our hurt should help the healing process. Alternatively, professional counselling is always a good option to look at, to effectively and confidentially address our insecurities.

If we constantly feel insecure about ourselves, the following steps will be helpful to overcome it and build a happier future:

- ✓ First find out and list all the prevalent insecurities we have. Then find out the causes of our self-doubts so that we know where to start fixing the problem. Do a self-reflection and write down which are the areas in our life where we lack confidence, or need assurance.

✓   Then go over the list one by one. Beside each item, write down an explanation why we feel insecure; recall how and when the insecurity was born; and then re-examine our feelings. Is our insecurity justifiable or is it just our fear magnified?

✓   Find out possible ways to change the insecure feelings, and what we can do to improve the area we are not confident about. Maybe we don't like how we look – so undertake a comfortable makeover of ourselves e.g. get a new haircut, change our clothes etc. Maybe we avoid meeting people because of our poor social skills. Do something about it. Read some self-help books or enrol in a class that will address our concern.

✓   Find support groups that will help us feel better about ourselves and our life. They could be our trusted friends, family members, an experienced counsellor, online groups, etc. Let them know of our struggles, and our sincere desire to change them. Having someone to help us change ourselves makes it easier than doing it all alone.

✓   Work on eliminating our insecurities one at a time. Hurrying up to defeat all of them at once will hurt our chances of getting over them. Be diligent and pray for success.

The point is, there is always something we can do to start building our confidence upwards, instead of wallowing in insecure feelings all through our life. True happiness, is locked inside all of us - waiting to be unlocked. We all have the right key, to open the doors to a secure future by getting rid of our self-defeating doubts and welcoming the real us!

Techniques to build self-confidence

First of all, we should know that self-confidence is a sense of belief in ourselves: in our physical, mental and emotional capabilities to handle, and face our problems. It is different than self-esteem or self-worth, which indicates as to how much we value _who we are_ as a human being, while self-confidence is about behaving confidently about our abilities and about _what we can do_.

Self-confidence is that intangible trait that separates the winners from the rest of the crowd. When we are confident, we even inspire confidence in others. Our level of self-confidence, shows in our body language, behaviour, and expressions.

Self-confidence building starts with changing our state of mind – our fears may ultimately be evident in some physical form, but they are present in our mind/ thoughts first. To overcome fear is the first step to building self-confidence. Our fear may even have its roots in some past negative experience - which no one is able to change or have any control on. However, our memory and interpretation of that experience is replayed in the present, over which we have total control.

Low self-confidence is self-defeating and seen as negativity. It covers areas like:

- having the tendency to cover up, justify or explain our mistakes rather than openly admitting we are wrong and correcting the course,
- dismissing appreciative comments with "oh, anybody could have done it", instead of accepting praises with gratitude and graciously,
- being reluctant to change,
- always doubting our capabilities,
- feeling like a victim of circumstances, and
- experiencing a lack of passion & difficulty in finding purpose of life.

Confidence building techniques are a great way to help us improve self-esteem, see our worth, and project a more positive version of ourselves. Self-confidence can actually be learned by practice. Here are some techniques:

- ✓ We need to remember our past achievements and think of them more often. Making a list, with various successes in our life so far, is a great tool to start helping ourselves to build our self-confidence.
- ✓ Deep breathing: take deep breaths whenever we are feeling lack of self-confidence. During such stress, the body seizes up and the tension in the shoulder & neck muscles deprive the brain of necessary oxygen – which is essential for reaching solutions. An extremely effective and quick relaxing technique is to inhale for a count of 4/5, hold our breath for count of 3/4 and exhale for count of 5/6, and then repeat this exercise 5 to 8 times.
- ✓ Face our fears: Feel the fear and do what we need to do in spite of the fear. This will help us deal

with our unfounded fears, by always remembering our strengths. Additionally, celebrate when good things happen to us.

✓ Act "AS IF": We can project being self-confident even if we don't feel so. Be spontaneous, respond effectively and faster, practice things that make us nervous and talk to friends when feeling insecure.

✓ Learn to laugh at ourselves: If we are not self-confident because we are afraid of making a mistake, allow ourselves to make mistakes and laugh when we do so. Humour indeed is the best medicine for building confidence and to get through even the most awkward situations. If we can get people to laugh _with_ us rather than _at_ us, it will do wonders for our self-esteem.

✓ Challenge ourselves. Take up an activity that we feel could be out of our reach. For example, if we are afraid of heights, sign up for rock climbing in a gym - there we are physically safe and we will feel incredibly better about our feat when we get to the top of the rock.

✓ Stop thinking about doing it - just do it. Over-thinking stops us in our tracks. Act on things rather than worrying about the future or dwelling on past mistakes. One of the best ways is to our turn negatives into positives.

✓ Plan ahead. If we know what to expect from a situation, we can plan in advance and this itself will make us feel more confident.

There is no doubt that self-confidence is a great asset. We can go out to touch the stars, and if we do fall we know that we will be able to bounce back again.

Ways to believe in ourselves again

"Believe in yourself, and the rest will fall into place. Have faith in your own abilities, work hard and there is nothing you cannot accomplish" – Brad Henry.

It is well known that if we want to succeed in life, we must believe in ourselves and our abilities because our *inner* faith will create our *external* results. We easily lose believing in ourselves when we encounter setbacks. When we lack confidence in ourselves, others take undue advantage of it, and do not take us seriously. Not many people live the life that they always wished to live – perhaps because they stop believing in themselves.

We are living in an extremely competitive and challenging world, where we start to doubt ourselves and our abilities when we meet with failure. But it is important to remember that a few failures are not the end. *A bend in the road is not necessarily the end of the road*. We must get back and face the situation.

Here are some steps to start the process of "believing in self":

1. <u>Accept our current situation:</u> The first thing we need to do is to accept our current life situation. We have to make peace with how our life looks at the moment, and what led to the situation that

we are in. Fighting with our situation will not do us any good. Being resistant is pointless. Only then will we have enough energy to face it, and change our life.

"If you tell yourself that you cannot, what can the only outcome be?" – Shad Helmstetter.

2. <u>Think about our past successes:</u> If we are feeling down and low, we can put ourselves in our past and think about the awesome things that we used to do, and get motivated again. While it is easy to recall the times when we failed or got hurt, it is just as easy to think about those times when we were successful. We can use our past to our own advantage.

"Every day is a new opportunity. We can build on yesterday's success or put its failure behind and start over again. That's the way life is, with a new game every day."– Bob Feller.

3. <u>Trust ourselves:</u> This is one of the most important things that can help us get our belief and confidence back. All the energy, power, courage, strength and confidence lies deep within us. Let us spend time with ourselves to access it, whether it be through meditation, journaling, mindfulness or such activities that help us gain trust in ourselves again.

"Everything in the universe is within you. Ask all from yourself." – Rumi.

4. <u>Talk with ourselves:</u> We are the ones who create who we will become. We do that every day by our daily beliefs and self-talk. It is really important that we talk to ourselves, and motivate ourselves. We do not ultimately need others' approval. We deserve our own self-approval and supportive self-talk.

"The brain simply believes what you tell it most. And what you tell it about you, it will create. It has no choice."

5. <u>Don't let fear stop us:</u> FEAR stands for False Evidence that Appears Real. More than anything else, fear holds us back from believing in ourselves again. We need to face our fears and not let them stop us from achieving our goals.

> *"Always do what you are afraid to do."*
> *– Ralph Waldo Emerson*

6. <u>Let us not blame ourselves:</u> We have to forgive ourselves for any failures or mistakes that we have committed in the past, and move on. We have to look at the future, and stop always living in the past. We need to be compassionate towards ourselves.

> *"A strong mental attitude can create more miracles than any wonder drug".*

7. <u>Maintain a Positive Attitude:</u> Having a positive attitude towards everything is the quickest way in achieving that belief and confidence in ourselves.

We should be thankful for whatever we are and whatever we have, besides always having a positive approach to see the good in the world.

"A mind is like a parachute: It works only when open".

8. <u>Seek professional help:</u> We can consult a professional counsellor who can help, support, and guide us. He can help us recognise our abilities, capabilities, strengths and skills, help us refocus on our goals keeping in mind our past successes. When we are full of doubt, he will believe in us and help us to believe in ourselves again.

"Counselling is an investment in ourselves and our future"

9. <u>Look forward instead of looking back:</u> There are going to be countless times in our life when we will feel down and wanting to give up. The voice in our head will tell us to stop and we will start doubting ourselves, but we should not listen to that voice alone. Instead we need to be strong and keep moving on and never give up on ourselves. We have to keep going, to eventually reach our destination. And when we do so, we will realise how much more powerful we have become.

"If you can't fly then run, if you can't run then walk, if you can't walk then crawl, but whatever you do, you have to keep moving forward." – Martin Luther King Jr.

10. <u>Follow life's natural flow:</u> When we learn to follow our life's flow, we will realise that life is

marvellous and precious. When we let our life guide us, it will shower us with its gifts and riches beyond our expectations. We have to accept the life we are given, deal with the pack of cards in our hand and learn to relax. Let us allow it to help us move in the direction we are meant to go, and we will find success.

"We all have different things that we go through in our everyday life, and it's really important to know that it doesn't matter what you face, you should believe that you are going to win at end of the day. You got to believe in yourself. You got to believe in that super power and know that HE is going to get you through it." – Kelly Rowland.

Overcoming Fears & Developing Self-belief

Let us try to recall, when was the last time we took a risk? Not really something major and life-threatening, but something that meant simply stepping outside of our comfort zone. Just recall a time in the recent few days or weeks when we did something that felt uncomfortable for us?

Quite often, we get too comfortable in life – we find a solid ground or a place where we feel safe to settle in. We are programmed to do it. That's how we all operate – look for safety and stay there. But in the present world scenario, it is imperative that we act against our programming to truly succeed, and find our own goals.

What's holding us back? Ultimately, it is almost always fear! Fear is the number one reason why people stay in their safety zones. It is why people don't start new businesses. It is why people stop advancing in their lives. It is why people hesitate to take bold decisions to face the uncertainties. But what are we actually afraid of?

After studying fear for several years and working with countless clients who were letting fear hold them back, researchers have observed that when it comes down to stepping outside one's comfort zone, there are really two things at work for most people: fear of success and fear of failure.

Fear of Success

Most people are not actually afraid of success, but rather of failing *after* the success. They are afraid they may not be able to handle it, and will fall much farther and harder than if they had never tried at all. They believe in the saying that it will be much more painful to fall from a 20-story building, than to fall from a roadside curb. It is the fall from the height of success that they fear, not the success itself.

When people say that they have a fear of success, it means that when they envision their success, they see the ways in which they will disappoint people, the ways they won't be able to handle the success, and the ways they will mess up their success etc. As it turns out ultimately, the fear of success is a fear of failure "in disguise".

Fear of Failure

Looking at the fear of failure, it is at the core of what is holding people back. Fear forces us to remain in our comfort zones. The fear of failure is not actually fear of failure at all, it is a fear of criticism. More than anything else, we are more afraid of being judged by others for our failures.

Now that we have somehow isolated this fear of criticism, can we do something about it? How do we conquer the one thing that gets in the way more than anything else - more than lack of skills, more than lack of knowledge, more than bad luck or anything else we might think of – how do we conquer fear?

How to Handle Fear?

It is easy for anyone to say that we just should not care what others think about us, what others say does not matter, does not define us, or has nothing to do with us etc. But the problem is, that it is not just the criticism of others - when we fail, we still have to face our harshest critic: that is ourselves.

According to the secret of successful people: we do not actually have to "conquer" fear, we have to "master" it. Mark Twain has said, *"Courage is resistance to fear and mastery of fear – not absence of fear."* Successful people are not people who conquered fear, they faced fear. They are the people who were indeed afraid initially, but did it anyway.

One of the most prevalent, persistent fear people have is of public speaking. It is something most of us do not do very often. But unlike many others who enjoy public speaking, many others get nervous before going on stage. Their palms sweat, they think about how they wish they had never agreed to do it, and they think of all the ways which can get them out of doing it. And then when they actually step on stage, within a few moments they have so much fun connecting to the audience that they forget all the fear – and just live in that moment. That is mastering fear.

A part of it is doing something over & over, and showing ourselves that we can do that thing. That builds confidence, and confidence is a formidable tool against fear. If we are not very good at something, we tend to fear it. What are we afraid of? Think about that for a minute and then when we have the answer, ask ourselves how often we do that thing. If we make a decision to face the fear and forge ahead with courage, we will eventually make courage a habit – and we will master that fear.

Here's an effective exercise that has been used to help people face their fears:

➢ Make five columns on a piece of paper.
➢ In the first column, make a list of the things that scare you the most.
➢ In the second column, for each of those fears, write down what is the absolute worst thing that could happen – if your fears came true.
➢ In the third column, write down how likely the worst thing is to happen.
➢ In the fourth column, write down how that fear is holding you back.
➢ In the last column, for at least one of the fears you have listed, write down how you are going to face that fear.
➢ Make it tangible – decide an "action" plan and a date" by which you will take that action.

And follow through! The results will amaze you!!

Everybody is afraid of something. The most successful people have mastered fear with courage and learned to forge ahead. Today, let us all make a decision to forge ahead with something in our life: a decision to face at least one of our fears; take a risk and get better at something we are afraid of; face our fear with courage and we will see payoffs emerging faster than we ever imagined.

> *"In order to succeed, your desire for success should be greater than your fear of failure."- Bill Cosby*

Get Over Fear and Make Positive Life Changes

Change is hard. It is even harder when it happens to be a big change – breaking up with someone we love, changing our job, moving house, starting our own business, or hundreds of such other difficult choices. Even if it is obvious that making a change will be beneficial for us, it still can be tough.

The following tips can help us move forward & make a positive change in our life:

1. <u>We will never have all the information</u>: We often avoid making important decisions – in absence of full information. Yes, it is essential to do our homework … but if we keep waiting for the crystal-clear answer to come to us, then we might have to wait a long time. At times, our *need for full information* can even be paralysing. Life is a series of guesses, mistakes, and revisions. Let us learn to take decisions, as per prevailing circumstances, have a mid-way correction, and move on.

2. <u>We need to trust ourselves</u>: We are worried that the unknown territory of the future – away from our comfort zone – will be too much for us to handle. Let us start believing that we have dealt with unexpected changes before also. So, why can't our confidence take us out of the present

situation this time too? We need to have enough courage to trust ourselves.

3. <u>The worst that could happen</u>? Most of our fears are created in our own head. When we actually sit down and think about the worst-case scenario, we will realise that there are actually very few risks that we cannot recover from. Let us ask ourselves - "What is the worst that could happen?" Once we realise the worst is not that bad (as we feared), we will be ready to crush it.

4. <u>Process of moving forward</u>: Most of the times, we are bothered about the end result. We worry that we might not make it to the finish line. "So-what" should be the question. As long as we are sincere, passionate and have put in required efforts - to the best of our abilities. Not to achieve our ultimate goal just doesn't mean we have failed. Failure is not a destination and neither is success - it is just as much about the process as about the result.

5. <u>Pursue new opportunities</u>: New choices rarely limit our options. In contrast, they open up even more options and newer opportunities - that we never expected in the beginning. At that point, our decision-making abilities will help us pursue the opportunities that arise on the path to our goal.

6. <u>Effort matters</u>: One of the reasons people don't make change is because they don't try. And they don't try because then it is easy to make excuses. If we try and fail, then we just failed. But if we don't try, then we can excuse it to our laziness. Let us get over it... Failure happens to everyone.

And if we actually try, then we can win a lot more than we think.

7. <u>Start with something manageable</u>: We certainly just can't climb the Mount Everest if we have not attempted other smaller hiking and mountaineering assignments. The top of one mountain is the bottom of the next. We can improve our skills and abilities so that we meet the essential requirements to get our dreams come true.

Certainly, we all are our happiest selves when we are in our comfort zone. Because we have specific skills and talents that match those circumstances

I am strongly in favour of increasing these happy moments by every human being.

We don't need to be a world changer today; we just need to make a small change in our own world!!

The Importance of Faith and Hope

Whenever we listen to any religious speaker we are sure to hear the word "faith", and then "hope" at some other times, while these two words are so commonly used by all of us. Even within the self-help activities and sessions, these two words are used on a regular basis. Still, it is an irony that most people actually do not understand them fully, or at least use them properly. It is important that we devote time to know and understand the meaning of these words, how they affect us or relate to us, and help us develop the ability to create and live the life of our dreams.

First, let us look at **Faith**. Faith is a term that is often used amongst religious groups, and far too often is followed by the word *blind*. In my honest opinion, we should never have blind faith - which is following something simply because someone else tells us to, or because someone else believes it to be good for us.

Instead, we must gather as much information as possible, about that which we are expected to have faith in. Only then we should be ready to place our faith in that something. We must then apply that information appropriately, and have faith that we will get results, if we walk that path. Faith is simply taking the time to gather relevant information and start moving forward, continuously paying attention to the results, and then making a mature, considered and educated decision.

As far as **Hope** is concerned, it is one of the most powerful words that we all need to learn to use. Hope gives us a purpose. It keeps us alive. It drives us, inspires us, and moves us to do more in order to have more. Hope is the driving force which gives us the confidence that things can be better, will be better, and we believe in ourselves. We should always hope for something bigger, better, more valuable, important and satisfying ahead in our lives.

We all must have faith and hope in life and develop a personal relationship to these two words. Together, these words move us forward: faith in our ability to improve our life, and hope for something better. Our mind's thought processes need to align, enabling a fine balance between faith and hope. This is why it is said that both faith and hope are essential for our successes in this life.

Dictionary defines Faith as confidence or trust in a person or thing, or a belief not based on proof. It is the substance of things hoped for, and the evidence of things not seen. While Hope is defined as an optimistic attitude of mind, based on an expectation or desire.

Faith speaks for the now in life, while hope speaks of the future. We need both. So, we must have a basic mind-set of faith in order to receive what we ask from that super power called Almighty. We have to know and truly believe that what we "set our minds to believe and focus on" is what will come to us.

Once we embrace hope and faith, we will begin to see the better and greater fruit of the seeds of our thought process. We must begin depositing "hope" seeds into our life, since these planted seeds can be the catalyst for the roots, and the foundation of our walk on the path of life.

Without realisation, every day we plant seeds of our life – as our thoughts. To have good fruit from our seeds, it is critical to plant the right kind of seeds, and nurture them with better manure & care. Better results, outcome and success can be guaranteed only after earnestly putting in the right efforts.

From another perspective, hope structures our life in anticipation of the future, and influences how we feel in the present. Like optimism, hope creates a positive mood and feelings about an expectation, a goal, or a future situation. Hope influences our state of mind, and brings behavioural consequences that modify our present.

A hopeful individual handles disappointment in a different manner than a person who is not hopeful. Even if the present is unpleasant, the thought of a positive future can be a stress-buster, and can reduce the impact of negative events or disappointments. When we are optimistic about the future, it helps us to recognise that we are adaptable and capable. That enables us to reassure ourselves that we will get over the tough time, and have a positive outcome from any situation.

We also need to understand that our talents, skills, or whatever else we want to call it, will not get us to our final goals all by themselves. Sure, all this helps, but a wealth of research over the past few decades shows that it is the few other *psychological vehicles* that really help us get there. Importantly, these are: grit, abilities, optimism, passion, self-belief, inspiration, thoroughness, and HOPE.

The persons who have hope, have the will and determination that goals will be achieved, through a set of strategies at their disposal. Simply said, hope involves the will to get there, and different ways to get there.

We all know that life is difficult. There are many obstacles on the path with inevitable twists & turns, and just having goals is not enough. Hope allows people to approach problems with a positive mind-set suitable to success, thereby increasing the chances that they will actually accomplish their goals.

Let us learn to forget about our past failures and begin to live with abundant hope and faith. Let us begin to allow faith to grow strong through hope, and live in our minds. Faith and hope will truly work together for our own good.

Life need not be a *struggle* always – it could be *full & pleasurable* with time for fun & relaxation, and finally *an adventure*.

Life is meant to be celebrated, lived, loved, shared and enjoyed.

Life can be converted from helplessness to hopefulness through learned optimism.

<u>Authentic Living</u>

It has been felt that most of us are losing the connection to our original and authentic self. We are suffering because of our self-created fears, and are unable to move forward towards varied possibilities of achieving our true potential. We are forgetting the basic essential nature of our spirit, and are mostly in a state where we do not know who we really are.

During our hard times, we not only look at our own selves differently, but the world also from a different perspective. We look at the world through our filters of individual perception – our fears, doubts, beliefs, learned assumptions and living values - and assume that the world is actually *hard*. This is a wrong assumption, because when we feel happy and joyous the same outer world reflects that particular happy feeling back to us. It can thus be said that the world is just a mirror, which is reflecting our individual feelings back to us.

Most great men and women have grown the most from their greatest challenges. All challenges can be seen as opportunities and treated as experiences, whereby we clean up our acts and overcome our weaknesses. Opportunities can be converted into positive acts to transform ourselves for personal growth/ wisdom.

Sometimes, we are frightened to move away from our comfort zones. Clinging to safe shores of our life is, as good as being imprisoned by our fears. In reality, there is nothing to fear to venture out into the unknown spaces. There we will have the opportunity & possibility to test our inner true potential, and emerge as a stronger, wiser and experience-rich individual.

There is a famous saying that "*Courage is not the absence of fear but the willingness to walk through our fears in pursuit of an important goal*". Another saying is "*On the other side of our fears, we will discover our fortune*" (Hindi: *dar ke aage jeet hai*).

There are valuable gifts available to all of us, in terms of <u>making new choices</u> and <u>taking few chances</u>. All it takes is some energy, dedication and time to explore the real us, and discover our true potential.

Einstein has said: "*By doing same things, different results can't be expected. To have new results, we have to behave in new ways*".

We need to choose to travel on a path that involves living life on our terms, according to our deepest values, and highest ideals. Generally, we all spend time to plan our vacations, but do not plan our lives ahead! How ridiculous could this be? Will we continue to carry on like this or be willing to take some decisions "now"?

It is said that good judgment comes from experience, experience comes from making mistakes, and mistakes come from bad judgment. We need to grow from our mistakes. Our stumbling blocks can become our stepping stones, if only we choose not to miss the opportunities which our adversities and tragedies present.

We can choose to curse the darkness, or to have the courage to light a candle. Darkness exists in the absence of light! Similarly, cold is the absence of heat. We don't study darkness or cold, but do study light and heat. Happiness is absence of striving for happiness - we ought to decide to be & remain happy, instead of just saying we deserve happiness. We need to realise the importance of living fully and authentically, while we have the chance to do so.

The things that we value most during our younger years, become the things we value least towards the end of our lives. Instead of learning how to live, we could learn how to make a living. This can be done by detaching ourselves, observing our environment & thoughts, accepting situations & environment, and finally by reducing our expectations. This will develop our spiritual, emotional, mental and physical health.

Life can actually be compared to a river with two banks – named sorrows and happiness. When we move along the river, we will have to brush up against both banks, and the real test will be not to stay stuck on either of them for too long. Every life has its share of victories & defeats, and sad & wonderful times. But hardships, setbacks, painful times and sorrows do not last forever. Brilliant sun rays always follow the darkest of the nights! At the end of every tunnel, there is light!! Our sufferings can be reduced by taking full responsibility for all our actions and choices, and that will shape our destiny - to reach and live happier lives.

We are all unique individuals, with our own strengths and weaknesses. Obviously, there will be individual differences with others. We must learn to value these differences – keeping in mind and appreciating our own qualities – instead of worrying about the expectations of others, and competing with them. We can increase our self-awareness, by recognising our uniqueness, working upon our inner experiences, and appropriately evaluating our abilities & capabilities.

There will be no objective achieved, by cursing our destiny, or luck, or blaming external factors for the situations that we are currently in. We need to keep in focus, our own contribution towards that particular happening, and be willing to learn from that experience. We need to consciously and constantly convert our weaknesses into strengths. We need to realise, recognise and appreciate our own positive qualities and emotions that will help us in maintaining and strengthening us. All this will help us enjoy our living, and make our life purposeful & meaningful to cherish each moment to the fullest.

When we don't blame anyone for our physical or mental state, we empower ourselves and increase our inner strengths. Other's blessings get accumulated, and increase our positive _karmic_ account and power. We all have to have a purpose of our life, and what better or beautiful that purpose could be than to grow into a mountain, instead of shrinking to a grain of sand.

When we dedicate ourselves to excellence, the entire universe will support us – by almost putting the required wind under our wings. In reality, everything may not work out the way we want it, but if we keep doing our best, and letting Almighty (whatever name one would like to give) do the rest, we will be able to accept whatever be the outcome. We may not be able to know the reason of any happening at that moment, but in the long run it will be for our highest good.

All that is needed is our disciplined approach, and commitment to make wise choices. A farmer has to sow the seeds, and put in real hard work to tend for them in order to get a good crop from his fields. He cannot afford to just sit, meditate and pray for miracles to happen! Same is true for all of us!!

To live an authentic life, it is a choice and a decision. Ours.

Self-awareness

It is said that *"awareness precedes choice and choice precedes positive change"*.

When we move on the path of self-realisation or awakening, we encounter certain happenings and opportunities. These force us to make choices, which can dramatically alter our life forever. Such happenings could be in the form of some suffering, loss of life, illness or financial crisis etc. How we respond at such juncture makes all the difference on our future life. In fact, it determines our destiny.

Our feelings need not be avoided ever, since these are intrinsic part of our inner self. We must acknowledge them, when felt, and give them the desired attention, before reaching the stage of making a choice to either reject them, or respond appropriately. Take the example of our fears or doubts – when we deny their existence, they remain in the background and continue troubling us. When we confront them courageously, we overcome them – just as a shadow fades when brought into light.

What we resist will persist, and what we take care of will excel.

We all very well know, that no life is free from problems and challenges. These actually can make us stronger and wiser. We do have the choice to run away from them. Complaining that life is pretty hard, will make us *bitter*. The other choice is to embrace them, and become *better*.

It has been said that *"the true measure of a man is not where he stands in his moments of confidence, but where he stands at times of his challenges"* – Martin Luther King Jr.

The great men and saints have expressed that, to learn to live authentically and then to reach the highest of his inner goals and potential, an individual has to go through <u>four areas of stability:</u>

1. Unconsciously incompetent

At this stage, an individual is not only incompetent but he is also not aware as to why is he incompetent. Many individuals actually stay in this state during most of their best years. Such people also make no effort to reflect on their own conduct, the choices available, or the quality and nature of the choices they make, and what needs to be improved upon.

2. Consciously incompetent

At this stage, the individual is conscious of his incompetence, and willing to improve. He is still incompetent, as far as his skills are concerned, but at least he is aware or conscious as to what all he needs to learn. When such awareness increases, the person is ready to look at the *new* choices available to him. Once a new or better choice is made, it will lead him to positive changes.

3. Consciously competent

Following the principle that awareness precedes choice and new choices bring changes in his life, the individual is then in a position to move forward. He is competent enough with respect to his skills, and absolutely conscious of his attention being paid to do the right things, at the right time. He is now able to listen to the silent whispers of his heart, and willing to follow the suggestions of his conscience.

4. Unconsciously competent

This is the last of the stages where an individual is willing and devoted, has mastered the necessary skills, and attends to his daily routine mechanically – without any efforts or second thought. Things happen to him almost unconsciously. All his actions are part of his being all the time. He is fully engaged in the present moment, and is completely awakened.

Things that happen to us in our life, have no other meaning except what we attach to them. We shape the realities of our life through our thoughts, and the way we interpret & process the experiences of our lives. All pain and suffering usually comes from our individual judgment. As soon as we stop being judgmental, desist labelling things as "positive" or "negative", accept them as opportunities to evolve ourselves, our authentic life will transform. This will then become part of the process of creating the life that we choose.

> *"Life brings pain all by itself. Our responsibility is to create joy"* – M Erickson.

<u>Awakening our Mind</u>

An old saying – "If we don't know where we are going, any road will take us there".

Let us draw a circle and divide it into 4 quadrants. And write in these individual parts – "Mind", "Body", "Emotions" and "Spirit".

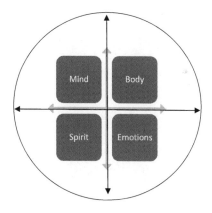

The circle here represents wholeness, which is the primary purpose of life, and the four parts need to be awakened – in order to understand our true self.

When we attempt to awaken our mind, we are exploring our core beliefs, assumptions, fears, and doubts that we have accumulated over the years. We are then able to be conscious of other higher choices available to us. From this it can be appreciated that, when we are able to awaken our mind, we will just be getting close to our wholeness by a meagre 25%.

A healthy mind can be more comfortable in a healthy body, so we need to awaken our body also. Caring to awaken our body means to follow regular exercise, proper diet, sunlight, fresh air, water, vitamins and all such essentials. This makes it 50%.

At the same time, it becomes important that we awaken and care for our emotions. When we are able to release our individually accepted negative emotions, we can move on with our life without being pulled down in any spiral. And simultaneously develop the positive emotions towards our wholeness in this segment. We then reach the 75% stage.

The awakening of our spirit is the highest point to reach. This could be different for different people – ranging from prayers, meditation, reading, listening to healing music, writing regular journal, volunteering for community service, caring for the infirm or terminally ill, and communing with nature or any such cause, that is larger than oneself.

The critical point to remember is, that all these 4 segments of our wholeness need to be addressed in parallel to each other. They don't have to be worked upon in isolation. Let's also remember that all this cannot, and does not have to, be achieved in a single day or a week or a month. We should just make sure that each day we do *something* to live our true life, and on the path of reaching our final destiny – however insignificant it may appear.

Any journey has to begin with a first step! If we don't act on life, life will act on us. Therefore, a commitment has to be made to ourselves to integrate all our activities in such a balanced & beautiful manner, that life starts looking worth living – for ourselves as well as for others.

It is true that happiness has always been a work which is best done deep within us. It is not about chasing greater *net-worth,* but about developing a greater *self-worth.* It is not about having more money, but about having more meaning. It is not about being successful, but about being significant.

With these qualities, it will be possible for us to create lasting values in this world. It is definitely a sign of maturity to love what we have, instead of worrying about having what we love.

Life can then be seen as a beautiful blessing.

And every single day, that we wake up, will become a gift to be celebrated.

We will, in the next note, know a little more about the stages of self-awakening.

Stages of self-awakening

According to scriptures, there are 7 established stages of self-awakening:

1. Living a Life of Lies

This stage is also called living an un-authentic life - which means living our life as per expectations and desires of _others,_ instead of _on our own_ terms. We basically hand ourselves over, and thereby our destinies, to those others who themselves have perhaps not been able to achieve true awakening, and are thus not in a position to guide us on the right path.

2. Reaching the point of Choices

Once we realise that we have been living an un-authentic life, and decide to be more authentic with respect to our inner voice, we come across loads of choices. These choices could appear confusing and difficult, but by proper analysis - using our knowledge, paying appropriate attention, being conscious, and processing through them would help us to select the best option available at that point of time. Once a decision is reached, complete responsibility should be on us, and on us alone, rather than any kind of blame on another person, or the circumstances.

3. Seeing the world with a new set of eyes

When we live with our choices, we start seeing the world with a separate and new set of eyes. We will then realise, that there was lot of hidden (or sleeping) power within us, and be able to discover the truth about enormous joy and happiness of this beautiful & wonderful world available to us.

4. Seeking guidance from Masters

This involves seeking and searching for teachers, to explore the different paths to learning. We seek answers to many questions that now surface and which have confused us, because of our limited knowledge, understanding, or learning capacity.

5. Transformation and Rebirth stage

This is the most challenging stage, when our inner self presents itself in some so-far unknown ways, and our world begins to change. Our perceptions about the world start changing. It is same concept as a caterpillar transforming into a butterfly, escaping the darkness of the cocoon.

6. The Trial stage

This stage comes after all lessons meant to be learnt have been learnt, and our greatest gift is just around the corner. Just like prior to any great victory, there is always a big test to examine how we react or respond at such times. We have to choose to be courageous, in order to move ahead on the path which will determine our destinies.

7. The Great Awakening of Self

This is the final destination – the stage of enlightenment. The next step is to share our learnings, after being completely transformed from living an un-authentic life of lies, to a stage when we start living on our own terms - authentically. We now uphold our values fearlessly, spread love, affections and positivity with an empathetic attitude, besides respect for all beings.

The ideal of faith in ourselves, is of great help to us. If we were more extensively taught in our beginning years to have faith in our own self, then with due practice, a very large number of the evils and miseries would not have been there.

"Whatever we think, that we will be: if we think ourselves weak, weak we will be; if we think ourselves strong, strong we will be; if we think ourselves impure, impure we will be; if we think ourselves pure, pure we will be", said Swami Vivekananda.

The seed is put in the ground, and then earth, air and water are placed around it. The seed does not become the earth, or the air, or the water. Following the laws of nature, it assimilates the air, the earth and the water to convert itself into a plant. Similarly, we must assimilate the spirit of others around us, and yet preserve our individuality to grow according to our core values and laws of growth.

Healthy Eating for Wellness

It is a normal saying that "We are what we eat, how we exercise, how we sleep, and how we interact with our environment". These variables ultimately determine the condition of our physical self. And our physical self, of course, greatly affects the capacity to express ourselves on other levels of our being.

The link between immunity and longevity is getting stronger. Most of us know that we should eat right because it can help us maintain our ideal weight, avoid many health problems, greatly improve our mood, and generally improve our wellbeing. Still, many times our diet is full of processed foods, packaged meals, sugary and/or salty snacks, and takeaway food. Research confirms that an unhealthy diet can even lead to mental health disorders such as ADHD, Schizophrenia, and Alzheimer's. The sooner we change our eating habits, the sooner we can do our part to lessen the burden of ill health on ourselves, our families, and our society.

It is also a fact that for just about every dietary tip one "expert" offers, there is usually another "expert" offering contradictory advice. Since diet is such a central part of any wellness program, we need to act as intelligent consumers of the information available to us by: studying it, analysing it, and making up our own minds about what is right for our bodies, lifestyles and food preferences.

Chronic stress, such as prolonged job insecurity or a difficult marriage or unhealthy habits, takes a toll on many aspects of our health. And, our lifestyle plays a crucial role in the proper functioning of our immune system. We need to look at some of the major factors to strengthen our immunity: guard against stress, quit smoking, do regular exercises, avoid antibiotics, develop positive emotions, socialise, fresh air breathing, sleeping appropriately, and of course watch what we eat.

Some tips for healthy eating

We need to examine how our diet is enhancing or undermining our overall wellness – and what we need to change. We may encounter many obstacles to implement the changes, but we will have to work through these in a deliberate manner.

> *Eat foods that are as close to the raw (unprocessed) state as possible.* The fresh fruits and vegetables are shown to have more of the helpful nutrients our body needs, and can absorb better than packaged, de-natured foods with ingredients (mainly synthetic chemicals, with supplements added).
> *Eat mindfully.* This involves not only eating slowly (so that our stomach has the requisite time to send a message to our brain that it is full), but also focusing on the food. For sure, our television, phone, computer, and other such devices should be turned off or not be in our hands at eating time.
> *Be sure to eat good breakfast.* It is the most important meal of the day, and numerous studies show that

kids who eat breakfast perform better at school, while adults are able to maintain their right weight.

➢ *Have enough protein.* Protein is the basic building block in a healthy diet. It has an important role of cell repair, cell regeneration, hormone production, and blood sugar management.

➢ *Control fats!* "Bad fats" such as the trans-fats found in most takeaway meals, processed foods, margarines, biscuits, and snack & fried foods should be avoided. These increase the risk of heart, stroke, and other "killer" diseases. "Good fats" include mono-unsaturated fats as found in nuts, walnuts, avocados, seeds, fatty fish and flaxseed, and hence strongly recommended.

➢ *Eat a variety of foods, but aim to feel just satisfied rather than stuffed.* "Portion control" strategy can be adopted by making it a practice to eat on smaller plates.

➢ *Enjoy the foods we love occasionally.* Instead of saying that any food is completely off-limits, we can try to eat a little bit of what we love as an occasional treat. We may indulge sometimes only, while maintaining our healthier habits as a regular lifestyle.

➢ *Eat when hungry.* Instead of eating all through the day, we could wait to eat when we are actually hungry. However, if we get too hungry, our blood sugar may swing wildly causing intense/ unhealthy cravings. A moderate hunger is the answer.

Exercise as part of Wellness

It is a well-established fact that exercise is an integral part of any weight management program. It is an excellent tool to boost our strength, stamina and flexibility. It means more power to our lungs and heart. At the same time, it is also true that it may actually play a very small role in the entire process of getting into shape. Lifestyle modification is equally important to stay fit and healthy.

The goals of any exercise regimen could be manifold - to run a marathon or do a triathlon, want to remain fit to enjoy a variety of activities in life (including to be able to keep chasing our grandchildren around the garden!), or perhaps just about losing weight. By keeping in mind our current fitness level, and having clarity on our goals, we will be able to modify the components of our exercise program.

There are, generally speaking, 3 kinds of "standard" components of any exercise program: strength/ resistance, aerobic/ cardio, and flexibility training.

- ❖ The physical training for strength/ resistance part helps us improve our lean muscle mass to fat ratio, builds and tones our muscles, and protects against bone loss. It includes walking, jogging, push-ups and lifting weights.
- ❖ The aerobic/ cardio exercises burn calories, work off unwanted fat since these involve the large muscles which contract and relax repeatedly, boosting

heart rate and breathing, providing oxygen to the muscles, and accelerating cardiovascular endurance.

❖ As we age, our muscles get shorter and tighter when not used, make us vulnerable to injuries and contribute to neck, shoulder, back, and balance problems. Stretching and <u>flexibility</u> helps to reverse that trend through repetitive performance of exercises which stretch elastic fibres surrounding muscles and tendons.

To help attain the regularity and continuity that we need from our fitness efforts, here are a few additional strategies which we can consider:

➢ *Keep a record of milestones*: In fact, it's a great idea to put our goals onto paper in the first place, as a reminder of what we are going for, and later, how far we have come.

➢ *Supplement our efforts with music we like.* Not all situations may support this, but some music devices can go many places and help us to relax.

➢ *Get a team of supportive people together,* who can help us improve our efforts, when our self-motivation and energy levels might be low.

➢ *Be flexible.* Life needs to be taken as it happens. We might have planned for a yoga class one day, but end up taking a walk instead. It's ok, since the point is that we are still moving. By being *compassionate for ourselves,* if we miss a day, let us consider it "no big deal" – since it is nothing compared to the long-term regimen we are committing to.

> *Reward*: And for extra motivation, let us *not forget to reward ourselves* for achieving our fitness goals.

If our calories intake is higher than what we can burn during the day, then the exercise is not going to bring fruitful results. Simple 30-minute walk can bring great results, as it raises our heart-rate by making us breath faster, feel warmer and burn calories. Sitting for long hours is one of the main causes of obesity and life style disorders like diabetes, hyper-tension and heart ailments.

Remaining active throughout the day is therefore important.

Exercise should be treated as a lifelong endeavour, something that is central to a well-lived life.

Time Management and Wellbeing

To understand our larger relationship with time, we have only to look at how we talk about it. Consider this –

Spanish say: "Time/ clock *walks*" (they believe in lots of walking in their daily life);

Germans say: "it *functions*" (obsessed with everything functioning perfectly);

French express: "time *marches*" (typical of the troop marches at war); and

English say: time in general "runs", as in "running out" (they love running).

Any guesses on how we Indians generally talk about, or regard time?

The entire world views time as a precious commodity in their respective perspective: we can "buy time", live on "borrowed time", or try to "save" time. If we don't manage to organise ourselves in relation to it, we are said to be "wasting" time or "spending" too much of it on something unimportant.

We all occasionally give excuses such as the following for not being prepared/ or reach on time/ or being ready:

"I just don't have time". In fact, each one of us has just 24 hours a day, seven days a week. How we choose to spend ours may not be actually working well, or as desired is a different aspect. Our priorities are all mixed up.

"I am overloaded". Yes, we probably are overloaded with lower-value things we chose to do, which obviously get in the way of our high-value, high-priority tasks.

"I am not disorganised, just too busy." If we have to justify as to how organised we are, chances are that actually we are not.

"I am late because I was held up". Late is late, regardless of any reason - whether traffic was too much or whatever. The hard truth is that we just didn't leave or plan to do things early enough!

Is it very difficult to appreciate that *now* is the future that we promised ourselves last year or last month or last week? This *now* is the only moment that we will ever really have, again.

We could go on and on. It can be said that those who don't have control of their time also do not have control of their lives - they are not living effectively or with much satisfaction. On the other hand, when we are organised well, we will experience these benefits coming to us:

- ✓ Greater productivity and efficiency
- ✓ Reduced stress
- ✓ Enhanced opportunities for advancement
- ✓ A better professional reputation

✓ Increased opportunities to achieve important life and career goals.

Moreover, with effective use of our time, we will be able to avoid the sad consequences flowing from these aspects of poor time management:

➢ Missed deadlines
➢ Poor work quality
➢ High stress levels
➢ Poor professional reputation and career going nowhere
➢ Inefficient work flow.

Managing our time better is, a proven way to increase our overall wellbeing.

I have read the following in a book, and would like to repeat:

❖ Time is slow, when we wait.
❖ Time is fast, when we are late.
❖ Time is deadly, when we are sad.
❖ Time is short, when we are happy.
❖ Time is endless, when we are in pain.
❖ Time is long, when we feel bored.

Every time, time is determined by our feelings and psychological conditions, and not by clocks. So, make a nice time, always.

We will learn some techniques to manage our time, in the next note.

Time Management Techniques

Let us examine some time management techniques, we can implement in our life.

There is a pre-requisite task to do - and the task is setting of our goals. When we know where we are headed to, and what we want to achieve, we will be able to prioritise tasks according to their importance. Failing that, we could end up - being able to tick off a large number of tasks as done, but realising at the end that they were all low or no priority ones, far away from the important ones!

We all are quite familiar with the fine art of goal-setting and use our own methods to do it. It is further recommended that it can work better when we start using a <u>master list in conjunction with a daily list</u>.

A master list is a paper-pad onto which we record all the possible notes, activities, action items, etc., say for an entire week while the daily list is a single sheet of paper onto which we plan a realistic number of key activities for a particular day alone. These two lists become easy to use, once we get the hang of these.

Some suggestions for the master list:

➤ *Maintain one master list.* We can have things from our work and personal life all mixed up on our master list. It will be easier to manage with a single system and we will feel less fragmented as a person.

➤ *Write down thoughts and then forget them.* Whenever newer ideas occur, we can jot them down on the master list so that we don't lose them, and continue keeping our mind free to focus on other tasks at hand.

➤ *Keep space provision in the list.* Leaving lines between entries and/ or plenty of margin space will help ensure that we can make notes without cluttering it up too much.

➤ *Make the master list for a longer period – at least a week.* The master list is not to be written every day or two! Items can be added or deleted, as required. And the previous week's master list should be filed for future reference (at least for beginners of this practice).

➤ *The master list is just a brain dump.* When things are written onto the master list, there is no priority assigned; we merely jot them down as thoughts/ tasks come to our mind.

➤ *Do write some details, and not just points.* Certain details are crucial to be written - e.g. the venue/ time for an appointment; solution presently in our mind to avoid any later confusion.

➤ *Have a mind-storming session at end of the day.* Take time to empty out as many thoughts as we can from our mind. This will free us to have a good work-life and personal-life balance.

➢ *Refer to our master list before ending the day.* Look for items that need to be scheduled for the next day, and put these onto our daily.

➢ *Evaluate weekly performance.* We can then transfer items not yet completed to the next week's master list.

➢ *Keep our list handy.* By keeping our list handy, we can re-schedule tasks appropriately, despite interruptions that can often happen.

➢ *Morning hours are most productive.* Since our productivity is at its best in the morning hours, getting one or two high-priority tasks done will make us feel good about our whole day, and reduce pressures later in the day.

In combination with the master list, it is also recommended to have a daily list which is drawn up from the items on our master list. Its purpose is to guide us to do the most important, high-priority tasks in a timely fashion, and to work on other not so urgent or important tasks, as time and circumstances allow.

Some suggestions for the daily list

➢ *Start to draw up the list the day before.* While the master list is prepared on a weekly basis (at the end of the week), it is best to write the daily list at the end of the day before. We need to keep in mind how much of our next day will be genuinely under our control, with various meetings, appointments, deadlines, or other commitments we already have. We should leave some spare time in our day to take care of unforeseen demands on our time.

➢ *Prioritise 2 biggest tasks.* These tasks will provide 80 percent of the value of all the tasks listed and therefore it is a good strategy to build the rest of the day around these two tasks. Our aim should be to complete at least one task early in the day, and a second one by noon time.

➢ *Try to plan the daily lists so that items are not transferred to the next day's list.* If this is not done, it will make us feel like we are not accomplishing much, or using our time well. If items are regularly transferred, it means that we are over-planning, or are unrealistic, or are disorganised.

➢ *Take breaks between tasks.* Statistically, our concentration cycle is of 90 minutes, after which we need a short break. This could be something as simple as getting up to get a drink, a brief walk around, or doing a short but pleasant task from the daily list. This will help us keep ourselves fresh, focussed and productive.

To summarise, it can be said that good time-management is good self-management. It is about living life on purpose, and choosing our activities & tasks in accordance with our larger purpose and goals, to manage the many distractions and interruptions, and to stay focused on those tasks with our full attention. Managing ourselves well through time is satisfying, high-performance-inducing, and career or life facilitating.

Get started today, for a better life ahead!

Status check of our life

In the present fast-paced age, we are "online", and checking our gadgets almost all the time (smart phones at least – with it's now established drawbacks and negative effects on our personal & social life, anxiety, self-esteem, and increased instant gratification attitude). In the process, we overlook the essential *"status check"* to be carried out on our motivation levels, and balancing of our emotions affecting our lives. By adopting such a status check on a more regular basis, we will be able to overcome & avoid a number of pitfalls in our life, and to achieve overall happiness & growth in our relationships.

We are living in a world which is constantly becoming competitive. We have somehow learnt to be critical and judgmental of others, and more of ourselves. This, many times, leaves us dissatisfied with our own performances and we are almost never contented so as to enjoy the life in its simplest form, leave aside the success of others. Our ego comes in between our rejoicing.

We need to start with making little improvements in our daily life. This can come through adopting the attitude of acceptance, and being less critical. The first step in the right direction will be self-acceptance as to who and what we are. We need to develop the ability to look at ourselves, and understand our own nature well. This will enable us to look where we can improve, instead of wasting our time and energy feeling guilty or regretful of our past actions. Acceptance of others, and the environment will then follow with much less efforts.

All this is achievable by keeping a check on ourselves, observing our motives, watching our thoughts & emotions, acknowledging other's good doings, seeking continued support through expressions of profound gratitude, and living a life with mindfulness – the "NOW" of our life.

Sometimes in our lives, each one of us feels that life is empty and we simply exist with no happiness. Such a situation can indeed turn dangerous for some people, and many may feel that the easiest way to get rid of their problems is by taking some harsh actions, including the extreme act of committing suicide. They find it very difficult to realise and apprehend that suicide is not the solution to their problems, however big they might seem to be. We must not surrender and feel weak, but instead should learn to face them head-on and find solutions. We ought to fight our problems courageously. Life is very precious – no one can afford to lose it just because the current problem seems to be unconquerable, as of now. We should learn to take and treat them as just a temporary phase of life.

There is an essential need to treat and celebrate life as a coveted trophy, which is maintained by polishing it and taking appropriate care of it, instead of letting it rot or vanish. We need to remember the responsibilities on our shoulders - of all those who need to be taken care of by us - and provide for their welfare and well-being.

Our thoughts are the propelling force within us. Let us fill our mind with the highest thoughts, speak them to ourselves, hear them day after day and think them moment after moment. We should not mind failures and struggles – they are natural. If we fail a thousand times, let us make a sincere attempt, one more time, to get up and achieve what we actually want to achieve.

Human beings have the power to concentrate. We can all concentrate upon those things that we love, and it is only natural that we will love those things upon which we concentrate our minds. We will then be able to control our mind instead of it controlling us.

The beauty is that concentration can be improved by developing the power of detachment. The power of the human mind is limitless. Regular and regulated breathing is the start point that puts our body in a harmonious condition, and it then becomes easier to reach the mind.

With passage of time and proper practice, we will be able to learn that nothing in this universe has the power over us, until we allow it to exercise such a power. We are the masters of our thoughts and thus our mind – not the other way around.

__What is Difficult__

It seems easy to be in another person's contacts list,
but difficult to get a place in someone's heart.

It may be easy to dream every night,
but difficult to sustain and fulfil our dreams.

It sure is easy to judge the mistakes of others,
but quite difficult to acknowledge our own.

It may be easy to forgive others,
but quite difficult to seek forgiveness.

It is definitely easy to frequently say "I love you",
but pretty difficult to demonstrate
it in your actions every day.

It sure is easy to criticise others,
but difficult to accept and improve upon our own faults.

It is easy to just keep thinking about improving,
but difficult to put our thoughts into action.

Understanding various Emotions

All human beings have certain emotions and feelings. Emotions are instruments of our survival. In fact, the human race would have vanished long ago, in absence of emotions. Emotions are indeed quite rational, instead of just being positive or negative, and help us achieve our goals.

Every emotion has a hidden component that brings in changes in our physiology, attention, perception, beliefs, and behaviour. Even the so called "negative emotions" are useful and do us a great favour, since they are the signals urging us to change how we normally handle things. By knowing when and how to deploy our emotions, we can live better with ourselves, and with others in this world.

Some of the emotions that generate unpleasant or uncomfortable feelings are: anger, fear & anxiety, shame & guilt, envy & jealousy, regret & disappointment, confusion & frustration, sadness and grief. All these are physically and emotionally unhealthy for us. Hence, we normally suppress them, even take medicines for overcoming them, and criticise ourselves beyond reasonable limits for feeling in the manner we feel under their influence!

Let us *briefly* understand these:

Anger

Anger can be seen as an ultimate loss-of-control emotion, perhaps because it triggers actions which are against our norms of care and courtesy. If we know what we deserve, and someone else sees things differently, it raises anger within us. Our heart rate increases, we start to sweat, we think about all the things we could do to set the other person straight. Related matters of safety, civic sense and practicality suddenly are forgotten, and we are unable to contain our enhanced physical energy. Anger motivates an individual to *take action*, unlike most other negative emotions which encourage us to *avoid situations*.

Fear and Anxiety

Fear is our appropriate response to signs of threat, and prepares our body to escape danger. Fear stimulates what is about to go wrong - and how to get out of the situation – i.e. our "Flight or Fight" response. When we are fearful, but can't directly address the threat, our fear takes the shape of anxiety. Anxiety can improve the performance of some people, who have the power to process it appropriately. It makes people energetic and vigilant. Research proves that anxiety not only preserves life, it is essential in all kinds of situations which require caution and self-discipline.

Shame & Guilt

We as human beings are able to progress because of the social structure that we live in. Society living requires us all to adhere to the established social and moral norms. When any such norm is violated, we need a way to pull ourselves back toward appropriate behaviour. That's when the emotions of shame, guilt and embarrassment arise, to make us self-conscious and feel uncomfortable. This discomfort leads us to turn deep within ourselves, in order to examine and analyse, what led to such a situation and what we need to fix. It is a well-known fact that people learn from their own mistakes, but it can happen only when it is acknowledged that something went wrong in the first place.

Envy and Jealousy

It is true that much of our successes depend on our relative status in society and resources. Also, our happiness is greatly influenced when we compare ourselves with others. If we are not as good as those around us, a combination of envy and jealousy brings in the discomfort. Envy and jealousy appear to be similar, but these are psychologically different. Envy is a longing for what another person has, while jealousy brings in inferiority complex in us. Envy can have destructive consequences, as well as some benefits. To reduce inferiority, envy encourages us to improve our successes and standing – by enhancing our persistence and performance levels, and even emulating the person we envy.

Regret and Disappointment

Regret sets in when we think about what *could have been* the possible outcome, if we had done things differently. It helps us to analyse and understand our past doings and actions. It boosts learning and planning. Regret also motivates us to fix whatever mess we have caused. Regret arises when an outcome is worse than *if we had acted differently*, bringing in our personal responsibility, while disappointment arises when an outcome is worse than *we expected it to be*, highlighting our powerlessness. Sharing personal regrets can make us humbler (as humans, we all make mistakes), and it shows that we care about the repercussions of our actions. Disappointment has its advantages too - it attracts sympathy and support. As a result, others become more helpful toward us.

Confusion & Frustration

When we encounter an unexpected outcome from a situation, wherein we had multiple options offering almost similar and reasonable benefits, it brings in an element of surprise. And when perception and logic are not consistent, we become confused. When confusion persists for long, we become frustrated. Frustration motivates us to work harder, shakeup our mental faculties and fight to address the uneasiness.

Sadness and Grief

It is unthinkable not to experience sadness and grief after any personal tragedy. Sadness comes in response to a real or potential loss, and motivates us to change things. Sadness makes our thinking more concrete and rational. It also makes us more sensitive to social norms, and functions as a signal to others that we may need help. While prolonged sadness can even lead to depression, it can be a healthy response to difficult life situations. Time is the biggest healer for sadness and grief. It is strongly recommended that a person should cry and let the inner sad emotions flow out when he/ she is in grief. That makes things easy for their expected functioning in daily life. It will help them face the real world, as destined for them. Though nobody wants to have grief by choice, it is one of the biggest growing experiences we can ever have.

So, while experiencing our emotions, it is important that we learn to accept, face them, develop our coping mechanisms appropriately, and try to have a good enough balance between the suffering and our handling abilities – to live a life full of happiness – the one we desire and wish.

__Wellness Dimensions__

Wellness involves proper integration of our various well-being states: social, emotional, spiritual, environmental, occupational, intellectual and physical. Each of these states act, interact, and significantly contribute to our quality of life.

Social wellness is our ability to relate, connect and interact with, and contribute to the common welfare of other people in our world, rather than to have a closed mind and think only of ourselves. This means our ability to

- ✓ establish & maintain meaningful relationships with family, friends and peers,
- ✓ respect ourselves and others,
- ✓ create a positive social support system,
- ✓ live in harmony with others from diverse cultures, backgrounds and beliefs.

Emotional wellness is the ability to understand ourselves, and cope with the challenges that life can, and will, always bring. Our emotional wellness gets strengthened with our ability to acknowledge and share feelings of

- ✓ anger, fear, anxiety, sadness or stress; as also
- ✓ hope, love, faith, joy and happiness etc.

It also involves having an optimistic approach, enjoy life despite its occasional ups & downs, disappointments & frustrations, besides accepting our mistakes for necessary corrective action, and to learn from them.

<u>Spiritual wellness</u> is essentially required to achieve and establish peace & harmony in our lives. We can contribute to our spiritual wellness, when we

- ✓ develop and practice consistency between our values and actions,
- ✓ realise a common purpose that binds humanity together,
- ✓ strive for a state of harmony with oneself and others, and
- ✓ are tolerant of the beliefs of others, rather than becoming intolerant.

It includes meditation, prayer, yoga, mindfulness or other specific practices, leading to compassion, capacity for love, forgiveness, joy and fulfilment.

<u>Environmental wellness</u> is the ability to recognise our responsibility for the quality of our environment and make a positive impact on the air, the water and land. We can significantly contribute, and minimise any harm to our environment by

- ✓ trying to live in harmony with the earth's natural resources,
- ✓ understanding the impact of our interaction with them, and

✓ protecting ourselves from environmental hazards – such as air pollution, ultraviolet sunlight radiation, chemicals, noise, water pollution, and smoke.

Occupational wellness is our ability to

✓ derive fulfilment from our work/ jobs or our chosen career fields,
✓ achieve and maintain balance between work and leisure time,
✓ address workplace stresses,
✓ build better relationships with co-workers, and
✓ contribute to make a positive impact on the organisation we work for.

Since our occupation takes so much of our time, it is important to do what we love, and love what we do, to have personal satisfaction and enrichment in our life.

Intellectual wellness is our ability to

✓ open our minds to new ideas, concepts, and experiences,
✓ seek challenges and reach for solutions,
✓ improve our skills that can be applied to personal decisions,
✓ engage in stimulating mental activities,
✓ expand our knowledge to discover our true potential and
✓ involve in group interactions for the betterment of society.

<u>Physical wellness</u> is our ability to

- ✓ maintain a healthy quality of life,
- ✓ develop and maintain endurance and flexibility,
- ✓ build muscular, bone and cardiovascular strength, and
- ✓ get through our daily activities without undue fatigue or physical stress.

To take care of and improve our well-being states, we need to adopt healthy habits (balanced diet, exercise, sufficient sleep, routine check-ups, etc.), and avoid destructive habits (smoking, drugs, alcohol, etc.).

The feeling good factors lead to psychological benefits of enhanced self-esteem, self-control, determination and a sense of direction.

Our Mindset – growth or fixed, & Behavioural Change

Mindset is defined as a mental attitude, that determines how we interpret and respond to situations in our life. Mindsets are all about the beliefs about our most basic qualities, beliefs about the world, and beliefs about what is possible to change, and what is not. Researchers across the world are attempting to figure out why some people achieve their full potential, and others don't. The key is not just our ability, but whether we view ability as something inborn (which must be demonstrated) or something flexible (which can be developed).

It was claimed by some philosophers about four decades back, that an individual's intelligence is a fixed quantity which cannot be increased. Today this appears to be brutal pessimism, because modern research has now proved that with practice, training, and appropriate methods, we can manage to increase our attention, memory, and judgment to become more intelligent than we were before.

Research has shown that we can develop our brains, just as a muscle - by putting in the right efforts. People who do that with persistence - despite many obstacles - can be termed as having a *growth mindset,* rather than a *fixed mindset,* and they enjoy significantly more success than their fixed-minded peers.

Let us attempt to define and compare these two kinds of mindsets, and then see the benefits of developing a growth mindset.

The fixed mindset

For people with a fixed mindset, intelligence is stagnant. And a fixed level of intelligence leads them to certain ways of living their life:

> *They avoid challenges:* obviously, the basis of any challenge is that it is something difficult. Since success is not necessarily assured, the fixed–mindset people don't generally take on the risk of failing, which in turn can negatively impact their self–image. They stick with what they can do well.

> *They give up easily in the face of obstacles:* they think in terms of why to waste time searching for a solution to a problem that they are ultimately going to be incapable of solving? Rather, they look for excuses to explain why the external forces were simply too powerful, forcing them to give up.

> *They do not put in effort:* they believe that there is no point putting in efforts, because even with practice, they will still only be "ok" and not "great".

> *They avoid criticism:* they tend to confuse negative feedback about a particular performance or capability, as if they are being criticised or being insulted. They don't believe that by avoiding

feedback they become starved of the information which could help them make positive changes.

The combined result of all this ego-protecting way of living life is, that fixed-mindset people often achieve less than their full potential.

The growth mindset

Persons with this mindset believe that intelligence can be developed, and the brain is like a muscle that can be trained. As a consequence of this belief, they have a desire to improve. They will typically do this in several ways:

➢ *They welcome challenges:* they embrace them, knowing that when they come out on the other side of them, they will be stronger and have an improved version of themselves.

➢ *They keep on in the face of setbacks:* they are not discouraged by external obstacles, because their self-esteem is not tied to how successful they look in others' eyes. They see "failure" as an opportunity to learn, no matter what the outcome is.

➢ *They see effort as necessary to master skills:* rather than avoiding effort as pointless, they realise that efforts are absolutely necessary in order to grow towards mastery of the skills they wish to have.

➢ *They welcome criticism and negative feedback:* they treat criticism and negative feedback as "vital information" - which they regard as a reflection about their current capabilities, and integrate the same with other useful comments – knowing that through them, they can change and improve.

Benefits of having a growth mindset

We can experience the following important advantages, when we believe that our abilities are malleable and can be developed:

- ✓ *We become oriented toward actual learning* and become smarter by putting in required efforts.
- ✓ *We are encouraged to try things, and to keep on trying* by allowing ourselves to be challenged by problems.
- ✓ *We embrace mistakes and setbacks* by understanding that errors and setbacks are an inevitable part of learning – so instead of fearing them, we welcome them, capitalise on them, and grow from them.

With a growth mindset, we get better at doing things, and generate positive feedback for ourselves. Once we reach that stage, we are encouraged to learn and improve still more, and finally make dynamic strides in our performance.

This results in the final impact that *we are predicted to be more motivated, and will have greater achievement,* when we adopt a growth mindset.

Controlling our Mind

Yogis, spiritual gurus, motivational speakers and meditation masters have all repeatedly talked and preached about the benefits of "controlling our mind". The prime purpose of our lives, as has been reinforced in us from time to time, is to attain happiness and satisfaction in whatever we do, work for the overall benefit of society in order to make this world a better place to live and leave for our next generations, and finally lead to some level of salvation of our souls.

We all know that when we start any exercises or any other physical activity, it is somewhat painful in the beginning. Even sitting in one posture for a little longer time is difficult. Same is true for the mind also – it can be quite uncomfortable in the beginning – as it tends to move around, and we are unable to concentrate. As is true for our bodies to adapt to the new regime, our mind also needs to be controlled, instead of letting it wander.

Small steps – like reducing expectations and accepting the realities of life - will motivate us to progress in the right direction of accepting the inevitable changes happening all around our lives, and to develop awareness of our inner strengths, happiness and wisdom. It will also enable us to learn how to use our thoughts, words and action in our everyday living to reach our desired destiny.

To keep our mind away from the monkey style chattering throughout the day, a simple practice is to follow this:

First thing every morning,

- ❖ if we can find a reason to say "Yes, it's *going* to be a beautiful day",
- ❖ and every day we find a reason to say "Yes, it *is* a beautiful day",
- ❖ and every night we find a reason to say "Yes, it *was* a beautiful day",
- ❖ then one day, looking back, we can say "Yes, it was a beautiful *life*".

Life is primarily about managing ourselves with the people, circumstances, happenings and environment around us. Success or failure of all our relationships is dependent on how we handle these. It is essential to understand that our determination, and not simply desires, is the first step towards making things happen.

This very <u>determination</u> will help us to keep our minds under control, rather than *just desiring* things to happen in a particular manner. We can control the functioning of our mind, and train it slowly so that it starts behaving in a much calmer way to keep us happy, satisfied and positive.

It is advisable and important to set certain goals of our life, so as to be able to measure life by our achievements and live a meaningful life. Setting up and then achieving Specific, Measurable, Achievable, Realistic and Time-bound (SMART) goals will always give us immense satisfaction. As time passes, we age and circumstances change, our planned goals need to be reviewed and modified. At times, we will face failures too, but that should not deter us from planning and taking life in our control.

Practicing meditation techniques is a sure way to calm things down, to be able to reflect on what's happening in our daily life and how we are developing as a human being. We can then also contemplate and work upon our weaknesses, convert them into strengths, and overcome obstacles to achieve happiness. It is perhaps giving ourselves, enough time and space to keep our minds relaxed and peaceful.

This state will provide us enough understanding and inspiration, instead of getting busy with unwanted thoughts clamouring our minds. With passage of time, we will be able to control our minds and remain positively committed to become the person we have always been wanting to be.

At this stage, it is most relevant to recall the saying >>

> ➢ *"Keep an eye on your thoughts, they become words;*
> ➢ *Watch your words, they become action;*
> ➢ *Keep an eye on your actions, they become habits; and*
> ➢ *Watch your habits, they become destiny".*

So, by adopting positive thoughts and intentions at the beginning of each day, we will bring in happiness and satisfaction in our actions at the end of the day.

Let us also accept the fact that though not all thoughts can be controlled, it is definitely possible to choose the thoughts on which we want and wish to act upon.

By thinking positive, keeping hope and faith, believing in self, being thankful for all acts of kindness, maintaining small gestures of love, empathy and understanding will always have a great impact on our overall satisfaction and give us the precious peace of mind. A controlled mind will also automatically step-in to help us in any adverse situation.

Our conscious mind will eventually understand that we are the master, and under no circumstance we are letting any laxity when self-discipline is concerned. Our mind has extraordinary powers; each mind is connected to the universal mind and thus can be in actual communication with the whole world. Now if every individual mind is in a state of self-control and concentrated on all good things, we can all imagine the benefits of such a disciplined approach, when the mind and body act upon each other in a positive manner. Indeed, a blissful living is achievable...

As normal humans, we all spend a lot of our resources (time, energy and efforts) to control people – at home and/ or at work place - and also the environment around us. The end result is almost known to us in the form of messed up relationships and resistance from those others.

If our desire is to control, then why not start at ourselves by controlling our own self... our thoughts...our mind... and our actions. This can be best achieved by taking a few steps backwards and many steps inwards, where we will find a big world waiting to be controlled by ourselves, and none else. Our urge to control will be far more fulfilling, and possible, instead of wasting time in controlling others.

So, how about making it a conscious choice to have "positive thoughts" in an effort to being in control of our minds at all times? And a controlled mind can be our best friend…with peace and contentment within…

The value of being an active listener

The greatest human achievement is to learn to speak our native language. Many of us are further trained by family and school to "speak properly", but less emphasis is typically placed on "listening properly". In life, generally speaking, most of us wish and desire to be the life and soul of our social setup. We wish that people find us interesting, and remain around us. For this to happen, one of the important things to develop is that we become a "skilful listener".

There are proven social and professional benefits of active listening. In order to cultivate active listening skills, these points can be followed:

- ➢ *Check our body language*: By making appropriate eye contact, sitting/ standing relatively straight, and oriented toward the speaker. We need to have an open body posture, and convey openness to what we are about to hear. Crossing arms in front of our chest is definitely a big no.
- ➢ *Apply the 80/20 rule to the conversation*: We should listen 80% of the time and speak 20%.
- ➢ *Ask open questions to gain proper understanding*: Compare these two sentences: "Did you react angrily when ...?" versus "How did you respond to...?" The second style gives the speaker much

more scope, to reflect on his/ her feelings before answering.

➢ *Use "minimal encouragers" to draw out the speaker*: Using short phrases such as "Yes", "I see what you mean", "Umm", or "Tell me more" etc. shows our interest & involvement, and serves the purpose of encouraging the speaker to keep talking.

➢ *Reflect back to the speaker occasionally*: Use the powerful tool of paraphrasing (what the speaker said in a condensed, non-judgmental form) and reflections of feeling and meaning. If we intervene non-judiciously, or too soon, or too often, we might completely break the speaker's flow!

➢ *Remember and recall what the person said*: If it enters from one ear, and is out from the other, how deeply could we be listening?

In today's digital world, the focus is on quick responses, and we can easily lose sight of the advantages of the gracious & unhurried act of deep listening. True listening is not just the *passive* act of hearing, but the *active* act of engaging the brain, concentrating, and adding comprehension. Through this, we achieve the following:

✓ It shows respect for the speaker, and thereby has immense capacity to build relationships, from work to social to intimate connections.

✓ It is the key to communication, as it is at least the half of any verbal exchange.

✓ It is very healing for the speaker, when he is genuinely listened to.

✓ It has immense power to help resolve issues.

✓ It improves decision-making, because we gain necessary details and perspective to make informed & intelligent choices, that helps find solutions.

✓ Attentive listening also allows us to "read between the lines", so that camouflaged information can come to the fore, giving insight and appropriate understanding of the real issue.

✓ Active listening accelerates our personal growth, as we gain

    a. self-discipline (because we will not jump in with our own stuff),

    b. empathy (because we actively put ourselves in the speaker's shoes), and

    c. maturity (because we stop prematurely judging people and their situations).

Guard our time & life - One day at a time

If we had a bank, which credited our account each morning with Rs. 86,400 – with no permission to carry forward the balance from day to day – what would we do? How would we spend that money? Well, we all do have such a bank… called Time.

Every morning, time credits us with 86,400 seconds to use for whatever purpose we choose. Every night it writes off as "lost" whatever we have failed to use toward good purposes. It carries over no balances and allows no overdrafts. We just can't hoard it, save it, store it, loan it, or invest it. We can only use it!

There are few very interesting, meaningful and relevant things about time:

Nobody can manage time. But we can manage those things that take up our time.

> ➢ *Time is expensive.* As a matter of fact, 80 percent of our day is spent on those things, or people that only give us two percent of our results.
> ➢ *Time is perishable.* It cannot be saved for later use.
> ➢ *Time is measurable.* Everyone – the poorest or the richest – has the same amount of time: 24

hours every day. So, it is not how much time an individual has, it is how much he is able to <u>use</u>.

➢ *Time is irreplaceable.* We never can get back time, once it is gone.

➢ *Time is a priority.* We all have enough time for anything in the world, so long as it ranks high enough among our priorities.

I recall the following analogy from my childhood, inculcating in us to appreciate the importance and value of time. To understand the value of:

- ° 1 year: ask a person who has failed the final exam/ delaying his career;
- ° 1 month: ask the stress faced by the parents of a pre-mature baby;
- ° 1 week: ask the editor of a weekly newspaper;
- ° 1 day: ask the daily-wager who has no work & has a family to feed at home;
- ° 1 hour: ask the editor of hourly news bulletin;
- ° 1 minute: ask the person who has missed his train/ flight;
- ° 1 second: ask the person who just escaped a fatal accident;
- ° $1/10^{th}$ of a second: ask the person who missed the gold medal in Olympics.

Even when our life is not going the way we want, when everything seems to hurt, when we feel unhappy or bad about ourselves, there still is a wonderful place we can visit – in an instant. Our own mind! Not to run away from the reality, but to look at it from a different perspective. No words and no actions can hurt us there. No one can take away this beauty of the mind!

All of us know the feeling when our "to-do" list is longer than the hours in a day. Sometimes we get "stuck" - not knowing how to move beyond procrastination, to accomplish things. Here is a very practical tip that can help us achieve our goals:

"For the next few days, at the end of each day, we can make a list of the six most important things we need to do the next day, and number them in their order of priority. We then cross out each item, after finishing it, and go on to the next item on our list. If something doesn't get done, put it again on the following day's list".

This practical advice has been followed by many with amazing success. A little twist can later be added to it - don't just number the tasks in order of importance, but always put the hardest one at the top. This way we can tackle the most difficult item first, and once it's out of the way, our day ahead will be off to a good start.

We all can follow this advice! Before we go to sleep tonight, figure out what we need to do tomorrow and write down the six most important things we need to accomplish. Not only will we start tomorrow ready to go, but subconsciously, we will also be working on those six projects while we sleep. Then, follow the advice and knock those tasks out from hardest to the easiest.

Let us not let our life get massacred out by what appears to be an innocent killer – the time! We can stand guard.

And when we guard our time, we will directly guard our life, and our destiny. Because time is the stuff, that life is made of.

Time waits for no one!

Yesterday is history; Tomorrow is a mystery; Today is a gift of God and hence called "present"!!

Build our parachute - reclaim life!

For most of us, things go on straight forward most of the times in life, but then a sudden turmoil comes which leaves scars in our minds and hearts. When things seem to be going smoothly, we suddenly feel tired, or angry, or sad with many negative thoughts going through our mind. Our mind then creates imaginary scenes, which become almost like an adhesive, and we cannot dismiss them from our mind despite all efforts. When we focus on them, they lead us to feelings of confusion, sadness, emptiness and hopelessness, and we start losing interest even in such things that once used to give us pleasure.

These states of our mind entrap us, and we then carry on the dead weight of our past failures, unfulfilled ambitions, relationship difficulties, and unresolved arguments etc. We find it difficult to let go of the past, and keep on brooding about it, or worrying about the future leading ourselves to a state of "*painful engagement*".

We feel guilty, for not being able to: cope with our situations, achieve our potential, and enjoy life or feel happy. We also feel angry on ourselves, for not living-up to our own expectations. We unnecessarily compare things, events and people and then feel sad, jealous and gloomy.

All this comes from the negative – mostly irreversible and irrational - thoughts in our mind that either we are not good enough, or we did not get what we deserved. One negative thought leads us to another and then next, leading us to an endless downward cycle which depletes our energy. When our mood is low, it blocks our memory from accessing positive times of the past, and its affect is so strong that we continue to be caught in its tight trap.

To counter such specific instances, we have the choice and possibility of forgetting & forgiving the past - in order to live each present moment in a state of mind which holds us in a non-judgmental, kind and compassionate understanding. We need to tell ourselves emphatically that "*Simply because I am feeling low at this moment, does not mean that things have to stay like this, for ever*". It can be changed for the better. We need to learn to see the situation from a wider perspective, which will allow us to be aware of the pull of our old habits of negative thinking, and take appropriate action for ensuring better care of ourselves during such vulnerable periods.

We need to choose to treat ourselves with kindness, refuse to judge ourselves harshly, and stop criticising ourselves & others for the so-termed irrational or inappropriate emotions. We need to accept ourselves with respect, honour and love so as to reach a stage of relating to our little world with utmost compassion. It may seem hard and strange to have kindness and compassion for ourselves, but it is not undesired or impractical. Because: we can nourish others, only when we nourish ourselves; we can truly love others, only when we love ourselves; and we can be good to others, only when we don't attack or condemn ourselves.

This is the actual stage to take back few steps from feeling guilt, shame, fear and self-criticism, and instead listen to the quieter, wiser, different and more reasonable inner voice of the heart. The hearts' voice is always present within us, even in our moments of stress and unhappiness, but we tend to overlook it. When we practice kindness towards ourselves, it increases – almost like releasing an endless flow from a water-spring - openness, creativity, compassion and happiness, while dissolving the negative forces of fear, guilt, shame and anxiety.

Kindness arises from having an attitude of empathy towards all i.e. a deep, shared understanding of the other person's dilemma. We can do a good-intention deed for someone else; we can forgive ourselves, and therefore others; we can develop faith, trust, belief, empathy, compassion and acceptance of others, and ourselves. We can overcome unhappiness, fears, stress and decide to refuse being taken down a spiral funnel of negativity, so as to save our energies and life!

It is as good as saying, that while building the life of our dreams, we need to build a parachute for ourselves – in parallel - every single day, to be used when our life starts to become difficult, or begins to fall apart. This is for those emergencies, when things are likely to take us low, and then our parachute can hold us from falling further into destruction! We will then be able to land safely and rise again!!

We can reclaim our life!! It will be worth an effort!!!

Talents & Strengths

While there are many similarities between the terms - talents and strengths - there is a slight difference between them. Talents on one hand are not as build-able, as strengths are. Talents - as for a sprint racer for his running speed - can be improved upon, since the primary talent to run fast already exists in the person. Strengths on the other hand - like integrity, kindness, humility and optimism can be built even on non-existent foundations. With enough practice, good teaching, persistence and dedication, strengths can take deep roots within us, and help us flourish.

Talent is relatively automatic and individuals have almost no choice about possessing it. Strength, in contrast, is usually more voluntary and we have the choice of not only when to use and whether to keep building it, but also to acquire it in the first place. By devoting enough time, with conscious efforts and determination, most of the strengths can be acquired and further strengthened by any individual. Talents, however, cannot be acquired merely by a desire.

Another significant factor of strength is, that its display by one person does not weaken other persons in the vicinity. In fact, the others are often inspired by simply observing their worthy actions. Strengths and virtues thus create a win-win situation and we can all be winners, by developing and displaying them.

Philosophers, world leaders and spiritual masters from times immemorial have endorsed six clusters of prime virtues: Wisdom, Courage, Humanity, Justice, Temperance, and Spirituality. There are several ways to acquire, build and develop these core characteristics towards living a "satisfying life", and to bring ourselves abundance of happiness. Each of these prime virtues is briefly explained below.

> **Wisdom** covers knowledge that comes out of curiosity. Curiosity in turn, involves our flexibility about such matters, which do not fit our perceptions. Remaining non-judgmental, being non-critical and open-minded permit us to examine things from all possible angles. Then we do not jump to conclusions when faced with certain new and unknown situations in our life, and change the perspective of the entire situation faced by us, or others who are seeking our guidance to help them solve problems.

> **Courage** means our strength to face adversity. This includes bravely facing the threats, challenges, difficulties and uncomfortable situations through our intellectual, moral, behavioural and emotional determination without any loss of dignity. Maintaining perseverance, genuineness and honesty help us achieve our goals using a realistic and flexible approach.

> **Humanity** involves kindness and generosity, through our social interactions with friends, family, acquaintances and even strangers. It

becomes our habit to do good deeds for all others. We value close and intimate relations with others, love ourselves and allow our self to be loved by others. We have other person's best interests as our guiding force, and at times may even override our own wishes & needs. Both empathy and sympathy are important factors for practicing humanity.

➢ **Justice** displays our civic activities towards all others, and not confined merely for a one-to-one relationship. In our normal work environment, we always do our share of the assigned task with dedication and loyalty - in our individual capacity - and work hard with team-work responsibilities, when we are in a group situation. At the same time, we do not allow our personal feelings effect our decisions about other people, and we are always guided by larger principles of morality in our day to day actions. Same applies in our personal life situations.

➢ **Temperance** refers to the self-control we can keep to have a check on our desires, wants and needs, whenever so required by the situation. In the unfortunate event when something bad happens, we are able to regulate our emotions and feel normal even in those trying situations. By observing discretion and caution, we should not say or do things we might repent later.

➢ **Spirituality** is our emotional strength, that lets us connect to something larger and permanent in this world of ours. This includes our appreciation of beauty and excellence in all spheres of life – nature, art, science and in everyday matters. We need to have, an *attitude of gratitude* so that we always express our thanks and gratitude for life itself, instead of taking for granted all the good things happening to us. Faith, hopefulness, forgiveness and optimism represent our positive attitude towards the future life, while mindfulness ensures that we can sustain the happenings, here and now.

Mindfulness & Power of our thoughts

A strong impact is made on our health and overall well-being by what we think and feel, how we talk to ourselves, and what view we take about what is happening to us, and around us.

Mindfulness, in its simplest form, means to be able to pay attention to the present moment, without judgment and criticism. To the things that actually *"are"*. We then start to see the world *"as it is"*, and not as we expect it to be, or want it to be, or what we fear it might be! It consists of starting to focus our attention on our breath, as it flows in and out of the body. We are then able to observe our thoughts as they arise in our mind, and realise that these thoughts come and go on their own, like the wandering clouds in the sky.

Mindfulness is all about the present moment. Major discoveries are being made about the link between our thoughts, emotions and health since there exists a connection between worry, stress, anger, our attitudes & beliefs and blood pressure, heart diseases, discomfort, digestive system, confidence levels, and a sense of optimism about the situations we face.

Mindfulness enables us to see the world and our circumstances with greater clarity. We can then take, wiser & more considered decisions and actions to change those things, which we can, and need to. It helps us create deeper awareness to assess our goals realistically, and then to find optimum resources for realising those.

We cannot stop the triggering of unhappy memories or events, anxiety, stress, irritation, self-critical thoughts and judgmental ways of thinking, but can definitely stop what happens next, and how we respond. We can consciously, put a pause on the negative thoughts, and thus avoid the next cycle of those thoughts which leads us towards a downward spiral.

Mindfulness teaches us, to recognise such thoughts as *mere thoughts,* and not as reality. Then we will be able to simply watch them evaporate before our eyes, and feel a sense of peace and happiness. Our mind is capable of not only thinking, planning, analysing and finding solution to problems; it is also capable of being *aware* that we are thinking. And that is important.

Mindfulness cultivates open-mindedness to acknowledge that anxiety, stress, unhappiness and such other difficulties are not problems that need to be solved. These are mere emotions and reflect the state of our mind and body. As such, they cannot be solved; instead they can only be *felt*. Once they are *felt* i.e. acknowledged, and we make no habitual efforts to "fix" them, they are more likely to vanish naturally - once again like the passing clouds. As we observe our body sensations and thoughts, and then their next wave and so on, we can recognise these occurrences simply as impermanent, passing events. A sense of spaciousness and ease will arise, making us feel calmer, and our attention will have a sharper focus.

Having understood what mindfulness is, it is also relevant to know what it is not.

- ➢ It is not "positive thinking" – as many people misunderstand. In fact, it is not thinking at all, but includes paying attention to thinking - where the thoughts are treated as objects of attention, just like any other physical object.
- ➢ It is definitely not just another "relaxation technique" – it is a way of life that can be learnt – to enable us increase awareness, and to achieve freedom from our habitual reactions.
- ➢ Its practice does not mean going into a trance, since the attempt is not to leave or change the experience of this moment, but to be present within it.
- ➢ Mindfulness is not only for monks or priests – it is a way of connecting with the natural quality of awareness and presence, which all humans have.

As we learn and practice mindfulness, we will become more aware, and others around us are likely to find us as helpful, patient, open-hearted, non-judgmental and compassionate human being. Being more mindful and aware will ultimately help us to live and enjoy our life to the full! Need we desire more?

Mindfulness today, is one of the most talked about developments in human psychology, and innumerable researches are being undertaken across the globe to understand its positive effects and implications. If interested, the reader is recommended to refer to the invaluable material available on the internet and print versions (please be cautious and aware of the information-overload) for individual knowledge, consumption, development and practice.

Perseverance

If there were a single word, to describe what people need in today's tough times, as has been in the past too, it would be PERSEVERANCE.

A large number of people have persevered in the past, through incredible difficulties to overcome daunting obstacles, and risen above personal and professional challenges to be successful in their lives.

PERSEVERE:

- **P**ersist no matter what
- **E**ndure discomfort
- **R**equest help
- **S**teadfastly hold on to our beliefs and values
- **E**nvision victory
- **V**ery consistently keep at it
- **E**mbrace adversity as our teacher
- **R**efuse to give up
- **E**njoy and celebrate every tiny bit of progress!

An ordinary individual who has the strength to persevere and endure – in spite of overwhelming obstacles – is a person worth emulating.

The price of success is: dedication, hard work, and an unrelenting devotion to the things we want to see happening.

<u>Negative thoughts are like hurting stones in the shoe</u>

Each one of us has had a *stone in our shoe*, at some point in life. And those moments always troubled us a lot. Our nagging thoughts are like those stones or pebbles which weigh us down, irrespective of their number and size. Each stone arrives at different times and intrudes into our lives. They may be small and undetected, but they actually represent many unresolved thoughts, images and experiences. Some of these remain undetected for years. Others push, prod, and make their presence felt every day.

Some are stones of doubt – formed from a single thought that may have generated many years, months or weeks before. Some stones are lodged only in our work shoes. Some reside in our house slippers, under our bed. Unfortunately, some of them even travel regardless of where we walk, or run. Some stones are of fear, guilt, rejection or shame. Maybe not today, but they eventually arrive unannounced and usually at the most inappropriate time. And they always present some challenges.

To run the race of life at our most efficient speed, we must be free of embarrassment, guilt, rejection, uncertainty, indecision, confusion, fear, envy, anger, jealousy, impatience, frustration and worry – all negative emotions. All these pebbles – like troubling stones – can be lodged in any of our shoe. They cripple us. They destroy our relationships. They coax us into drug and alcohol addictions. They destroy our families, alienate our friends, besides ruin the true potential of our children, and physically take away precious years from our own life.

Any pebble can make us to quit, or respond to with complete indifference. Even the malicious desire for fame, fortune or power can turn into an undesired pebble in our shoe, if left undetected. Most pebbles stir up the past, cloud the future and keep the present to a blink of the eye. Like a small plant that comes out in a garden that's been freshly tilled, a pebble can reappear without warning or detection.

Taking preventive measures and removing them completely are our only options for a balanced life. To get rid of all stones and pebbles, we need to learn how to clear our mind of all the negative emotions, stated above.

__The Pregnant Deer__

This is a short story about a pregnant deer in a forest, who is about to deliver a baby. She finds a safe grass field near a flowing river. At the same time, dark clouds gather around and lightning puts the forest on fire. On her left side is a hunter with his arrow pointing at her, and on her right side is a hungry lion wanting to kill and eat her.

What will happen? Will the deer survive? Will she give birth to the baby? Will the baby survive? Will everything be burnt by the forest fire? Will she be killed by the hunter's arrow? Will she die a horrible death at the hands of the hungry lion?

The beauty of the story is that she just focuses on giving birth to a new life.

As a matter of coincidences, the hunter gets blind by the lightning, his arrow gets released – it zips past the deer and hits the hungry lion, the forest fire gets doused by the heavy rain, and the deer gives birth to a healthy fawn.

Let us have a quick check on the circumstances above, and ask ourselves whether the deer had any influence in the chain of reactions that happened to her and to her adversities right in front of her eyes.

Similarly, in our life also there are moments when we are confronted on all sides with negative thoughts and various possibilities. Some thoughts are so powerful that they overcome and overwhelm us. What we must avoid is to take our attention away from our goals. In contrast, we must remain focused on the issue at hand.

Maybe we can learn something from the deer.

The priority of the deer was simply to give birth to its baby. The rest was not in her hands and any action or reaction that changed her focus would have definitely resulted in death or disaster.

We need to ask ourselves: where is my focus? where is my faith and hope?

The strong persons know how to keep their life in order. Even with tears in their eyes, they still manage to say "I'm ok" with a smile.

Stress - as a matter of choice?

It could be quite a liberating and supportive concept, that if stress could be a matter of choice, we can as well *choose not to* have it! Indeed, what an option!! Most of us seem to have an endless to-do list, and rushing around it perhaps stops us from seeing the bigger picture. Actually, taking a step back from our daily schedules can help us simplify our lives…and maybe even help us to identify what we are missing, to keep us energised and fulfilled.

Most of us hurry through life going from one place to the next - focused on reaching the next milestone, making the next deal, running the next errand, believing firmly that we will never have enough time to do all the things we need to get done. Ironically, the same amount of 24 hours by the clock is available for each of us every single day, and hence all that matters is how best we utilise it. It is impossible to increase this time, so it is advisable that we set our priorities right besides improving our internal energy levels and enthusiasm to handle our challenges.

If our life - both professional and personal - is over complicated, we must accept that we are the ones who have chosen it to be that way. The society and the environment further tempt us to fit more and more things, people and processes into our lives, which quite often leads us to be stressful.

Stress impacts our thinking, feelings & behaviour, and may lead us to a downward spiral of negativity. To avoid it and experience a simplified life, we first have to learn to slow down long enough to see through all the clutter around us. As part of this process, it is important for us to commit to simplify it, and not hesitate - instead be willing - to even seek support from others.

Mostly, a lot of stress and the resultant anger in our mind or fear of failure, is based on our assumptions. We assume or imagine, that people are actively conspiring against us, and situations are going out of our control. This impacts our emotional, mental & physical strengths, and coping abilities. It strains our neurological system and heart to such an extent that our brain releases more stress hormones resulting in digestion issues, increased blood pressure, intense and negative responses besides affecting our all other functional abilities and faculties – mind being the most severely affected.

To overcome such stress effects, it is important to realise that our responses were mostly due to some of our own assumptions. We must give a chance to the reality to play its part. Patience comes as a big antidote to this unnecessary stress – so we must tell ourselves that we may be wrong in our anxious imaginings, and need to give a little more time to our thoughts, instead of jumping to conclusions. Any kind of diversion at those moments, will help us buy that extra needed time, so that the truth of the situation is also revealed, and we are in a far better state of mind to evaluate and arrive at reasonable conclusions.

Like a flowing river can be tamed to use its waters for productive use - through newly opened channels - our mind can be tamed to function in a productive manner – just by some self-effort. By regularly encouraging and cultivating our thoughts and mind, we can channel our speech, character, actions and ultimately our destiny. We can be the architects of our own future, by making intelligent choices of transforming our thoughts.

We all need to live rightly today by embracing the values of love, patience, compassion, tolerance, forgiveness, harmonious relationships, empathy, mindful meditation (call it by any name), and a positive attitude. Then the negative influences can be detected, well in time, and overcome through constant, dedicated and conscious efforts.

Meditative stillness allows us, to understand ourselves and the life with its challenges, simply by shifting perspectives. Our intellect survives on thoughts – positive or negative – and the choice is all ours. Let us clear our minds of all negative and stressful thoughts – for as little or long time as we can - and give ourselves the opportunity of hearing our inner voice. We need to stop looking towards others for authenticating ourselves. When was it that we last heard ourselves, in all sincerity?

There are individuals, who manage stress with very few or no significant health problems. These individuals are strong on:

> ➤ <u>Commitment</u>: having a deep interest and involvement in what is happening to us and around us, and having a set of important moral values.

> ➤ <u>Control</u>: having confidence to have the ability to handle destructiveness of a particular stressful situation, and be able to focus on what we can control, and not be distracted by what we cannot.

> ➤ <u>Challenge</u>: to have the ability to treat the stressful situation as an interesting opportunity for further growth and excitement, besides welcoming and accepting corresponding changes.

We must realise that we are the creators of the life we choose to live. At the same time, life itself is a series of choices, and being free from stress is just one of them.

We need to learn, the art of dropping our stress for a few minutes each day, and experience the marvellous affect it will have on our rejuvenation – before stress drops us!

We need to kill our stress, before it kills us!!

Deep breathing exercises and simple meditation skills help us, to avoid our unnecessary & avoidable stress, and successfully face challenging situations.

Regret or Learn from experiences & move on

As an individual, if we mostly continue to wallow in the past, it is time that we start learning from our experiences and move on…. Many of us spend more time looking *regretfully backwards* than *hopefully forwards*. We are constantly bothered and tormented by thoughts of "what if…" and "if only…".

Our past *is* important, because it has shaped us as to who we are today. The past is our experience, but regretting the decisions we made or what happened to us is pointless and a waste of our time. At the time when we made our choice, it seemed like the right one but now it looks different. We can spend some time, changing our present and future by making choices now. There is no point in saying "if only I had done that"- there was perhaps a good reason why we didn't.

The way to handle regret is, to accept the reason why we made our choice and understand that we have learnt something positive, even if it now looks like a mistake. It is only a mistake, if we have not learnt from it. Well, when things do go wrong – as they would many a times – it is totally natural and normal to spend some time going over what happened in order to understand it and learn from it.

We normally ask ourselves "was I to blame?" or "could I or should I have done something differently?" We learn what we can from such an eventuality, and then move on. But sometimes we can get so caught up in focusing on the losses and errors of our past, that we can't really 'get going' on our present or future.

If we are stuck in a kind of a fantasy world, we normally tend to think what life *would have been like,* if only that particular thing had not happened, or we had not made such a blunder, or those good times had not ended. And, of course that 'other life' has some sort of a glow and charm about it, which is so much more appealing than the actual life we are leading now. No wonder, we are consumed with grief for what we have lost, or have not been able to sustain. We seem to be out of our comfort zone! And that is awful & frightening!!

Constant regret about the past is termed as unprocessed grief. We may be experiencing it as anger or hatred – with ourselves or others – or shame, or self-blame or even blaming someone else for all this unfortunate happening in our current life, or going through any number of other negative emotions. When we lose what our lives 'would have been', it is very much like a bereavement, and grieving is a process by which we separate ourselves from what has gone forever and is irretrievable, before beginning to face the future again.

Regret, like grief, is a process that may take some time to wean off, but it does not have to continue forever. So, if we find ourselves caught up in bitterness and resentments of our past – even after a significant length of time – it is important to take stock, and see what can be done to free ourselves from that negative grip.

We need to examine, as to how badly it has been affecting our normal life and what are we achieving out of continuously living (or is it just surviving?) such a life. This calls for an immediate decision to liberate ourselves from the chains of negativity. Liberation involves interrupting the *habits* of regret, the automatic self-defeating thoughts, and developing a new *vision* of what the future can be.

We can learn to help ourselves, to let go of regrets and look to the future. By following some elaborate psychological modules, we can significantly ease our path to a life free from unnecessary regrets. This will take us into a profound and peaceful state of mind, which is the ideal 'learning state' for the brain.

It is possible, to learn and practice the methods that can help us:

> begin to categorise and sift through the disturbing events from our past,
> focus on the here and now including appropriate prioritising,
> identify what is "stealing" our present precious time and is it worth it,
> free up of our time, energy and enthusiasm for more control on our life,
> develop a wider perspective on what brings significance to our life,
> create a new purpose and meaning for ourselves, in line with our values,

- ➤ start to develop a plan for what we will do differently next time, and finally
- ➤ discover how we can make and live so much more of a life – happily and at peace – not only within ourselves but also with our circumstances and situations.

Regretting forever is never the way of living a life!

Learning from experiences and moving on is!!

Live our dreams

Our happiness in many ways, is directly connected to our "inner voice" that forever asks the question… "Are we moving towards our dream?" If the answer is "yes," then the hope breeds happiness. However, if the answer is "no, it's too late," then the pain may irritate our subconscious.

As part of a step-by-step action plan – that we can start implementing today itself – we need to ask ourselves some straightforward questions. This will enable us, to become our own guide to help us get the right answers, and to make relevant decisions along the way.

At times, we are unsure of what our dream might be – either because we are afraid to dream, or because we somehow lost our dream along the way. Then we need to start preparing ourselves to revive our dream, by doing the following five things.

> ➤ Experiential Preparation: Engage in activities related to our interests.
> ➤ Visual Preparation: Put up pictures of people, and quotes that inspire us.
> ➤ Idol Preparation: Read about and meet people we admire & who inspire us.
> ➤ Physical preparation: Get our body in optimal shape to pursue our dream.
> ➤ Mental Preparation: Read, study & gather material in areas of our interests.

This all means that, we are not leaving our dream just to chance. While no one can deny the power of such proper and thorough preparation, many of us still neglect to <u>act</u> on our own to truly live our dreams – for somewhat unknown reasons.

As part of this beginning, to discover and *live our dreams*, it is important to commit ourselves to work towards it and enrol support from others, if needed. We can start on a blank sheet of paper, and create the purpose of our life we truly want to live, supported by a clear sense of our simple decision to live it! Rest will be history!!

We can then move towards achieving our dream – one step at a time.

Make Happiness a habit

"Most people are about as happy as they make up their minds to be" wrote Abraham Lincoln. There couldn't be any disagreement on this. Happiness seems to be a habit as much as anything – a habit of attitude, a habit of responding to life, and a habit of action.

I have displayed a sign-post on my office board, which I noticed somewhere, and have been greatly influenced by it. It says: "*Happiness is available. Help yourself.*"

I love the words "help yourself", as if a bowl full of happiness is lying on my desk, like a bowl full of sweets, and all one has to do is to dip the hand in and take it. "Help yourself" means "take action on your own behalf." How meaningful!

I also draw a reference to the book titled "Happiness is a Choice" by Barry Neil Kaufman. The author and his wife had their third child, a boy who was diagnosed as autistic. At first, the couple was devastated – they thought their lives were ruined, and their child doomed to a hopeless future. But once they worked through their initial reaction to the diagnosis, they made a huge choice: they decided to be happy. They said to themselves: "We can let this situation drag us into depression and self-pity, OR we can decide to love our child, make a nurturing family for him, and have a good life together". They chose the latter.

Rejecting the advice of doctors to put the child in a special institution and move on with their lives, they completely redesigned their home, and their lives to meet the needs of their autistic toddler. He couldn't meet them in their world, so they decided to meet him in his. They sat on the floor and played with him, mimicking his shrieks, cry outs and wild gestures. Bit by bit, they were able to build rapport with their son, teach him new behaviour, and coax him further and further into normalcy.

The boy grew and thrived under his parents' unconditional love, patience, and teaching. It was a long and challenging process, but he finally graduated from high school and then college, with honours. And throughout those challenging years, Kaufman and his wife chose to be happy. They had made it their habit.

How do we make happiness a habit? By simply <u>choosing</u> it. Again, and again. Habits are formed by repeating the same thing over and over again until it becomes the normal way we behave. Scientists tell us that if we repeat something consistently for 21 days, it will become a habit – our generic cells actually get into the mode of new learning every 21 days!

> ➤ *Happiness is not a destination - it is a journey.*
> ➤ *Happiness is not tomorrow - it is now.*
> ➤ *Happiness is not dependency - it is a decision.*
> ➤ *Happiness is not who we are - it is what we have.*

A simple formula, to increase our happiness and make it into a habit is by increasing our optimism and hope. The key for this is, to first recognise the pessimist or negative thoughts and then treat them as if they were said by an external source, whose sole purpose is to make us feel miserable. Do we want to listen to such a source, or do we want to implement our own decision to feel happy?

Whenever we recognise that we have a pessimistic thought, we should dispute that unwarranted thought and argue against it using the ABCDE model:

ABCDE means:

- ❖ A – an adverse situation,
- ❖ B - beliefs that we automatically have when it occurs,
- ❖ C - consequences of the belief,
- ❖ D - disputation of that belief, and
- ❖ E - energisation that occurs when our dispute is successful.

We will be able to overcome the negative & pessimistic thoughts with our positive & optimistic attitude, supported by our decision to opt in favour of happiness, under all circumstances!

So, if we want to really feel the Power of Happiness habit, we should start by making happiness our new habit, and transform our little world to be a place worth living, and leaving for our next generations.

There is a common saying "If you don't move forward, you will move backwards". It is therefore imperative that all of us keep a target to steer our life towards a higher goal – of living happily!

An agitated mind vs
a serene mind

What we normally do on a daily basis, depends on the state and quality of our consciousness. We all can appreciate that when our mind is cheerful, we find every other thing as pleasant and cheerful. In contrast, when the mind is gloomy or sad, our outlook becomes miserable. Our moods, relationships, knowledge, productivity and perhaps every other thing happening around and with us is, thus dependent on different states of our consciousness.

Let us simply compare our life to water – when it reaches the boiling point, the evident agitation and chaos seems to be disturbing and increase the activity of the hydrogen and oxygen atoms that form the water. When the temperature comes down, we observe that the orderliness increases. Further, the same atoms appear to be forming perfect crystals when this water is put in the freezer. Similarly, if water is shaken in a pan the surface becomes agitated and reflections get distorted. When the water becomes still, the reflections become much clearer.

These very scientific principles apply beautifully to human mind: when there is so much activity in our mind, we feel disturbed, tired, say wrong things and also take bad decisions. When we are more settled and at peace within us, we are happier, more effective and more perceptive.

The state of consciousness, where mind is at peace, has been termed as the state of "knowingness" by many learned saints and yogis. Simple *knowing* is on the surface of the mind, while *knowingness* is at the depths of a silent mind. It resembles the difference of activity at the surface of an ocean, and activity at its depths. We also know, that a tiny movement at the depths of an ocean can create huge waves on its surface.

Experiencing the silence and serenity of our inner self will help us quieten our turbulent minds, and help and lead us to make our outer world become a better place to live.

Our attitude determines our altitude

It is a very common saying, that our life's success lies in our personal attitude. While it is not easy to accept this, the importance of making a conscious decision to be and remain positive for our health & life can't be overly expressed. The difference in our success or failure is, not on how we look, not on how we dress, and not even on how we are educated. It's actually dependent on how we think!

The power of choice is one of the greatest gifts we human beings are given. Each choice has a positive or negative consequence for us at some level. Our attitude toward life is the most important choice we make! Though this choice appears a simple one, many times it is much more challenging for most of us.

As an example, let's just think of the last time we were driving home from work. Driving is a relatively complex task, requiring many choices along the way – turn right, turn left, slow down, stop, change lanes etc. Still, driving home is successfully performed – almost subconsciously. Similarly, we make many other choices each day that we don't really think about: waking up, brushing our teeth, saying "good morning" to a colleague, eating our lunch, performing a repetitive job, and so on.

Subconscious actions are useful, most of the time. But we must also consciously choose our attitude, to control our results. Our ability to choose is a gift, and a huge responsibility. We can write the word responsibility as *response-ability*.

We have the unique ability to respond – which is a result of consciousness. But when we just react, it is normally an emotional and subconscious decision. Such reactions do not help us achieve the best results. When we simply react, our emotional instinct is in control, with little thought of the long-range consequences.

On the other hand, when we respond to a situation, we make a constructive and conscious decision. And when we respond, our brain is fully engaged and our self-awareness is high. We have the long-term consequences in mind. Choosing to *respond* instead to *react* helps organise our attitudes and our lives in a positive manner. Perhaps, that's why there are emergency *response* teams, and not emergency *reaction* teams! While we can't control what life does to us, we can definitely control how we react or respond to what life does.

In order to improve our life and change something about it, we should remember: "we cannot build a life that is better than what we believe we deserve". So, before we try to change our life, we should think about our attitude. Do we firmly believe that we deserve a better life? When the answer is "yes", then it becomes possible to take appropriate actions to achieve the desired change.

It actually does not matter what our past has been, we *do* deserve better! When we can confidently say out loud "I deserve this or that/ a better life/ job/ happiness/ success or whatever...then we can move forward and achieve it.

So, truly our attitude can and will determine what altitude we reach in life!

I can, I will, I believe... is my standard recommended prayer.

<u>Why sound sleep</u>

All of us are so less bothered about the fact that our sleep, and also its pattern, is getting affected due to increased stress levels of our daily life, and jam-packed schedules. Getting adequate sleep is almost becoming a luxury, rather than a necessity. Remaining awake till late night is becoming a habit – especially of the younger generation today - though even young parents are quite happy in remaining busy with their social network's updates. From the well recommended standards of approximately 8 hours of sound sleep for an adult, the trend is alarmingly dropping to about 5-6 hours a day. Sleep is no longer on our priority list. This sleep deprivation is adversely affecting our overall health and life.

Medically speaking, our body needs regular updates and appropriate controls over many internal systems, including hormone levels, insulin levels, immune systems, and even blood pressure. In absence of proper sleep, all these get affected and disturbed. A reduction of approx. 1.5 hours of sleep in a night has shown to have a direct impact on our day alertness, efficiency and performance levels by as much as 30+%. It has been proved that in-sufficient sleep results in:

- ✓ increase of our anxiety levels,
- ✓ irritability,
- ✓ frequent headaches, and
- ✓ short-temperedness

leading to serious health issues like

- ➢ hyper-tension,
- ➢ diabetes,
- ➢ insomnia,
- ➢ heart ailments,
- ➢ weight gain,
- ➢ infertility, and
- ➢ shortened life expectancy.

In biological terms, there is a gland called Pineal gland placed in our head which is connected to the sight nerve. This gland starts working, after it becomes dark and until two hours before sunrise, and produces a chemical substance called Melatonin. It runs in our blood stream and produces a vaccine that naturally protects the body from cancer. This gland cannot work when the eyes are exposed to light. When we sleep, we are directly initiating the gland to start its function. But when we stay awake till late night, we deprive our body from this natural vaccine.

Individuals can become prone to anxiety disorders because of lack of sleep, since their immunity system does not get enough time to build up the infection-fighting anti-bodies and cells. Even healing and repair of body tissues gets slow, resulting in frequent sickness. The kids can become hyper-active, inattentive and impulsive due to lack of sleep. It has been researched and proven that sleeping well during our formative years can ensure better mental function in our later years, and may be able to prevent age-related memory loss and the dreaded Alzheimer in old age.

Sound sleep of minimum 10 hours in younger children, and 8 hours during adolescence age allows the brain to consolidate learning's of the day, and improve their long-term memory. The most common sleep invaders are:

➢ excessive viewing of TV, and
➢ usage of modern day smart-phones, iPads, Laptops etc.

since their glaring screen lights throw-off our body's natural rhythms of sleep and wake cycles.

It is, therefore, very strongly recommended that we all put off using such equipment at least an hour before sleep, and see the amazing results when we will start getting proper and deep sleep on a regular basis.

Our food intake at night time, should ideally contain sleep-promoting substances like warm milk, and other carbohydrate-rich foods like nuts, banana, honey and eggs. Exercising well during the day is also a great help for sound sleep at night.

We all should attempt to maintain a regular sleep cycle – even on holidays as part of a healthy lifestyle. The results will be only positive on our overall wellbeing.

Saying "Sorry" and understanding its components

There are umpteen numbers of time, when one has said "sorry" – and quite often, if not most of those times, without understanding the real meaning of the word "sorry". A misunderstanding, a miscommunication, or an exchange of harsh words – in any relationship – can lead to resentments and regretful situations later. The two simple words, "I'm sorry" can result in such hard feelings to vanish – depending on how this expression comes out – it could be a matter of accepting responsibility, and not to lay blame on someone else.

Quite often, these words are said without it being a heart-felt apology – without sincerity and any humility. Just regretting the incident, does not actually mean an apology. When we make a mistake, it usually brings in our instinct to dig our heels in, take an undue or unreasonable stand and defend ourselves – for our action or words. We normally insist, that we were right and it is the other person who is refusing to see the real point, or the reason. Many times, it also happens that we recall all the earlier (past) times when the other person had supposedly hurt us. This is a direct attack on the other person, by implying that he/ she does not have any reason to complain when he/ she has been equally guilty in the past.

Many a times, the word "sorry" is uttered quite a number of times – more as a matter of polite behaviour than being meaningful. A person's egoistic self, also expects the other person to make the first move. Consequently, and with the passage of time, the relationship between two people becomes virtually irreparable, as none of the two sides are willing to "forgive and forget". Apologising for an incident does not mean, that we are wrong and the other person is right – it simply means how much we value the relationship with that person, compared to our ego.

In intimate relationships, people have also been found to bring in the entire relationship into question just in order to draw or divert the attention away from the one specific current instance for which an apology is "requirement of the moment". It so seems that the word "sorry" is such a difficult or hard word that using it and meaning it becomes so complicated.

If indeed "sorry" is being said, we ought to say it right and also mean it. The recommended rules of saying sorry, meaning it and accepting it could be summarised as:

> An apology should always avoid the word "but" (as in: "I am sorry, but you started this or said this and that…"). In true sense, it should never matter what went wrong before or what comes after. If we have hurt someone or done something wrong, and if we need to say sorry, we should say it with all humility and acceptance of responsibility – without any ifs and buts!

> The apology should never be conditional (as in: "If my words pained you then I am sorry for

hurting you"). Under such a statement, we are trying to say that the fault was of the other person (and not ours) and we are trying to make them feel better.

➢ Once someone has apologised, and this has been accepted, the matter should be treated as closed for ever. Let that matter never be brought up times and again – it will only keep on disturbing us.

➢ The apology should never be used to make the other person feel small – either in public or in private. Turn the page…Close the chapter… And, move on….

By taking stock of a situation and accepting our mistake, we go deep within our core and patiently seek course correction. We can then, grow up to look at everything from a different perspective and never ever repeat the past mistakes. We need to become accountable to ourselves and responsible for the way we perceive, feel, emote and act.

It is a truth that "to forgive" is a much bigger and tougher task than "seeking forgiveness" – it requires all the beauty of heart and wisdom of the mind to accept someone's sincere apology and forget that incidence. It may be hard to learn the art of "forgiving", but it is worth its value in terms of being wise, magnanimous and kind hearted. It directly increases our self-esteem and prestige manifolds, in the eyes of all those who matter in our lives and for whom we genuinely care.

Moving from Apathy to Empathy

Apathy in general, is defined as: indifference, lack of interest, or concern for others. More specifically, the disability to identify with others or feel their pain is the primary nature of those who are strong on apathy.

Empathy, in contrast, is defined as having compassion and sympathy towards others – to the extent of being able to relate with them and their pains. Empathy is, also the ability to understand or feel what the other person is experiencing or going through. It is the ability to step into the shoes of another person, with the aim to understand their feelings and perspectives, and then to use that understanding to guide our actions. That differentiates it from kindness or pity. Additionally, empathy helps build trust and encourages communication, while lowering conflicts.

Interestingly, modern research confirms that empathy can be taught and learnt. It is a habit we can cultivate to improve the quality of our own lives. The learning is not difficult and empowers us to emotionally connect with people around us. We can make empathy an attitude, and a part of our daily lives, and thus improve our own as well as the lives of everyone in our social environment.

As a <u>first step</u> to develop empathy, we need to be only curious and not extra inquisitive about others and their activities.

Curiosity expands our empathy when we talk to people outside of our usual social circle - encountering lives and worldviews which are different from our own. We should be, an interested inquirer instead of being an examiner!

To start with, we may set ourselves the challenge of having a conversation with one stranger every week, and see the results. All it requires is courage. Curiosity allows us to get inside the skin of another person, and makes us less non-judgmental, which is the most critical trait of an empathic person. By being non-judgmental, we can avoid jumping to conclusions and making such statements which may distress others - on account of our speech and expressions.

It is often seen that most people open up to others - with their personal issues and concerns - not only because they want, need or expect a definitive solution or an answer to their concerns, but because they want to use the listener as a sounding board, and help themselves sort out their muddled thoughts & emotions. As an empathic person, we may not agree with them but under no circumstance will we ever criticise them. Any criticism will make them withdraw. Instead, we need to listen to and engage with them without judgment.

As our second step, we need to challenge our own preconceptions and prejudices by searching for what we share with people rather than what divides us. We all usually have assumptions about others. That prevents us from appreciating their individuality. We need to shelve our assumptions and accept the differences.

Thirdly, we can expand our empathy by gaining direct experience of other people's lives, putting into practice the proverb: "Walk a mile in another man's shoes, before you criticise him".

There are two more traits required for being an empathic person. One of them is, to master the art of listening. It is essential, that we have the ability to listen to what is really going on within the other person, and to the unique feelings and needs the other person is experiencing in that very moment. An empathic person will listen hard to others and do all he can to grasp their emotional state and needs.

When it comes to listening, it is quite important to look and grasp even the non-verbal cues that will enable us to truly understand other person's emotional state of mind. It indirectly initiates an introspection to question our own thoughts, beliefs and actions. This will enable us to take steps towards building better relationships.

The second trait is to make ourselves vulnerable. Removing our masks and revealing our sympathetic feelings to the other person is desirable, for creating a strong empathic bond. Empathy is a two-way street, that is built upon mutual understanding, and exchange of important beliefs & experiences.

It may not always be easy, or even possible, to empathise with others but adopting good people-oriented skills and some imagination, we can work towards increasing our empathic attitude. Research further suggests that, individuals who can empathise enjoy better relationships with others, and have greater well-being through such an attitude in life. It indeed pays to be empathetic!

Calming our anxious minds

To be human and not being anxious, seems to be an impossible combination.

Modern life has brought us worries and anxieties in the form of strained relationships, unresolved past issues, uncomfortable working environments, fears of not fulfilling expectations adequately, financial difficulties, unhealthy diet, and excessive consumption of stimulants etc. Anxiety, worry, fear, and stress have been seen to be an integral part of almost every psychological problem faced by individuals in today's world.

Any person prone to anxiety can worry, be fearful, be stressed, or be bothered and feel anxious just about anything and everything. And such worry, fear, stress, botheration and anxiety can make our life hell. These are akin to taming and feeding *our inner wolves*, without even realising their impact on our overall wellbeing. Unless we learn to fend off and master the "inner wolves that eat us up", we will keep falling prey to all the fear, worry and anxiety reactions within us.

It is therefore very critical, that we learn to gain control over these habits, so as to lead a calm and peaceful life.

"To fear is one thing. To let fear grab you by the tail and swing you around is another" - Katherine Paterson.

Our fears, worry, anxiety and panic are all very demanding in nature and can turn our inner world upside down. All these, however, are not permanent. We will have to use our tools effectively, in order to manage these and discover what works best for us - under different circumstances. By remaining focused and maintaining calm, we can practice our learnt principles of awareness, understanding, kindness, compassion, perseverance and mindfulness.

We also must not forget, that it is sometimes normal to experience whatever scary anxiety symptoms we have, and when we realise how many other people feel the same way, we would start to feel as if we are just part of a club, rather than some sort of a freak or a lone-out-of-the-world person.

By overcoming fear and anxiety, we can generate the "spare capacity" in our life to focus on what we really want _to be_, and _do_. We all _do have_ what it takes, to find inner peace and _can_ change things by paying attention. Yes, it takes effort but we can imagine, visualise and appreciate all the rewards that it will bring in.

Is it not worth trying out to build our own tool-box?

Repeatedly reaffirming "I am happy, I am healthy, I am safe, May I be filled with love, light, peace and ease", will enhance our feelings of kindness and compassion, whenever we feel overwhelmed and distressed from anxiety and fears.

Amongst the anxiety and worry related problems, Generalized Anxiety Disorder (GAD) is most frequently observed – which means feeling tense and anxious much of the time over such things that should not normally bother us. When we feel like that every day, it quickly takes out the meaning from life, and each day just feels like mere survival. We then resort to, taking medicines and drugs before becoming dependent (and at times addicted too) on those.

Well, drugs are not the answer for the majority of anxiety conditions. In my experience, they can be useful only for a short term – until new self-management skills and new ways to manage our thoughts & emotions are learnt and effectively used – that are relevant in today's world, and our immediate environment.

Let us now learn some techniques for calming and controlling our mind.

__Techniques for Calming__ __& Controlling our mind__

In order to begin to address the issue of anxiety and worry, we need a tool that cuts off anxiety at the very source of its beginning. Quicker, shallower breathing is the first sign which triggers off all other anxiety symptoms. Deep breathing exercises, at all those times of worry and anxiety, can be used by every person because of their sureshot effect. By controlling our breathing, we can control the other anxiety symptoms.

When we purposely and consciously breathe-out longer than we breathe-in, our body calms down. This is hardwired into our nervous system, and the body cannot ignore its effects.

So, when we start to feel anxious, we should: (a) Stop, (b) Focus on the breath, (c) Take a breath in (to the quick mental count of 5 to 7), and (d) Then slowly breathe out (to the mental count of 9 to 11).

If we continue this just for one or two minutes, we will be amazed how quickly we calm down. This is referred to as "7/11 breathing" but the numbers are, strictly speaking, up to us – just as long as the out-breath is significantly longer than the in-breath. It could even be 5/8. This exercise is simple, and has intense effect on our mind and body. It can become one of our secret weapons against all sorts of anxieties – only if we practice it well! And the best time to practice is when there is no stress around, so that we are already good at using it when actually needed.

When we get anxious about upcoming special events (examinations, marriage, interviews), it has been noticed that just thinking about the event starts to cause physical responses – butterflies in the stomach, quickening pulse, palms getting moist and so on. This in turn, makes our body to become even more anxious in the actual situation, and so the vicious cycle continues.

But breathing in a relaxed 7/11 or 5/8 way (while thinking about the upcoming event) will calm down the association and prepare our mind to feel more relaxed - naturally and automatically - when the actual situation arrives.

Another symptom of too much fear or anxiety is, not being able to think straight. This happens because the emotional part of our brain "floods" the thinking part. When we are able to put our "thinking brain" in a working mode, we will be able to sail through the flood and in turn remain calm.

The easiest way to keep the thinking brain active is with numbers. We scale our anxiety from 1 to 10 – where 10 is the most terrified state and 1 is the ultimate relaxed state. When we feel anxious, ask: "What number on the scale am I right now? Am I at 8, or a 6 or …?" Just doing this will lower our anxiety, because it kick-starts the thinking brain, diluting the emotion and automatically making us calmer. If we scale ourselves at a 6 at a particular occasion, the 7/11 breathing for a few moments will bring us down to a comfortable 3 and we will be able to take control over the situation. This kind of scaling (also referred to as "grading") helps our mind to put a "fence" around it, making it more manageable, and forces us to think.

Fear, worry and anxiety thrive - when we imagine the worst. Imagination is also considered a tool to be used, but most of us, many times, misuse it to torture ourselves beyond need. As humans, our imagination has brought us to where we are today. It is a beautiful, unique part of us and a wonderful thing, but not if we use it to scare ourselves.

A negative side-effect of having an imagination is being able to imagine things going wrong. Some of this is actually useful at times - there really might be attackers or deadly sharks in the ocean ahead! But uncontrolled imagination is, a breeding ground for anxiety and fear that can spoil the otherwise happy lives.

Sometimes we need to be able to "suspend the functioning of the imagination" - Ernest Hemingway.

When we look at an upcoming event in our mind and imagine the worst outcome, it amounts to be the same thing as *using a hammer to paint a picture*. We must remember that, our imagination is there as a tool to be used constructively, and not destructively. By practicing imagining things going well, and also thinking about them to ultimately happen the way we want them, we will be calmer in the situation, and be able to make a much better use of our time & resources.

If we still continue to have negative thoughts, then at least we should attempt to "dilute" them as much as possible by imagining a positive outcome - in parallel to the negative one. Stopping negative thinking takes time and effort, but it is not impossible!

When we find, ourselves imagining awful things that are *likely* to happen, we can learn to monitor our thinking by starting to develop and practice our tool-box:

❖ Sit down, relax and do our 7/11 breathing.
❖ Scale our anxiety level, think about bringing it down to a 3 or a 2 or a 1.
❖ Imagine seeing ourselves in the situation we were dreading, but then also see ourselves being calm, composed, cool, and comfortable and things actually going well.

Doing all this will start to recondition our mind to feel calmer and more relaxed about upcoming events or situations which cause us anxiety.

Another method – called as the <u>AWARE</u> technique - is also very useful for regaining control over high anxiety levels and even panic attacks: It stands for...

➢ **A**: Accept the anxiety. Don't try to fight it. We need to know and remember that it would not kill us.
➢ **W**: Watch the anxiety. Just notice it, scale our level of fear and start to breathe longer on the out-breath.

➤ **A**: Act normally. Carry on talking or behaving as if nothing is different. This sends a powerful signal to our unconscious mind, that its over-dramatic response is not needed because nothing "that unusual or extra-ordinary" is happening.

➤ **R**: Repeat the above steps in our mind, if necessary.

➤ **E**: Expect the best. One of the greatest feelings in life is the realisation that we can control anxiety and fear much more than we ever thought was possible.

Readers may please also refer to the detailed write-up ahead under the heading "Anxiety".

Solo Parenting – modern day dilemma, compulsion or fashion?

Parenting in today's complex world, is more complicated than the present senior generation (people born before 1960) could ever imagine. Till about 50 years back, parenting was never looked at as an issue requiring any special skills – children just grew up without so much fuss, and in the company of their cousins as part of the large/joint family system. Both parents were, most of the times, available to their children – except those few who were in frequent transferrable jobs.

However, in the present scenario, we have a wide range of variations of a family. The joint family system has almost disappeared, and lately even the nuclear family is in a transition phase - showing all signs of a further break down. Divorce rates have seen a significant increase. Marital discords have increased, and tolerance levels have decreased.

Decision to discontinue an emotionally-not-fulfilling or a psychologically abusive relationship is not such a daunting or stigma–attached act today. Couples feel they are capable of looking after them-selves, and can handle their responsibilities well. They prefer to opt out of a negative atmosphere which is full of resentments, anger, hatred, sarcasm, fear, nagging etc., and look forward to creating a positive, loving and compassionate atmosphere for their life to be peaceful.

Any societal pressure to remain in an incompatible marriage, is a thing of the past. If we look at it in depth, it can be realised that for some it becomes a necessity, while for many others it is by choice. The ultra-modern concept of live-in relationships (prevalent in the western world for many years, and catching up faster within India as well) is not uncommon any longer, even in our conservative towns.

These youngsters are not really bothered about the marriage and its resultant commitments. They are even willing to go ahead and have a child (biological or adopted or through sperm or egg donors) that they are willing to bring up alone – if the situation so demands. They prefer to be a single parent, rather than entering into a life-long commitment with a person they are unsure of spending rest of their life. Having a *meaningful and mutually respectable relationship* is considered a better option by them.

This entire rapidly-changing socio-cultural environment, obviously brings in major challenge for the role and responsibilities of parenting to just one of the parents. Single parenting is a reality of modern times, and hence it becomes obligatory for all of us to look and deal with related issues in a pragmatic and empathic manner.

It could be a physically exhausting, mentally stressful, financially challenging and emotionally draining responsibility to shoulder & fulfil the material and emotional needs of the growing child. In absence of a family support system, this task could become enormous for the single parent. It could further become worse in view of the continuing conflicts, fights, blames & counter blames, ego games, custody battles / visitation rights etc. between husband and wife.

All this has a direct and serious impact on the child, and requires full dedication of the parent with whom the child is to be resident majority of the time (obviously, it is the mother in most cases). Such a parent would be required to meet the emotional and psychological needs of the child, arrange financial resources and possess all the mental strength to go through single parenting – as she/ he would have to play the role of a mother and father both. And this, by no means is going to be a comfortable or an easy task.

Ideally speaking, parenting would be best when both mother and father are involved to bring up their child together. But the unfortunate existence of an abusive or incompatible relationship cannot be the reason to tolerate the nuances of such an unhappy home where the child is likely to be more under harm and duress during his/ her developing years. A well-considered decision to split or continue such a relationship, will have to be taken based on facts, situation, circumstances & adversities experienced, and would be in order.

The challenges, and even stigmas attached, will have to be faced bravely and overcome by the single parent by sheer determination and taking them as opportunities to create an environment of a "happy home" for self and the child. There is no need to look at self as a failure; rather it should be taken as an opportunity to be happy, confident, independent to work, earn, enjoy, develop our support systems, be with friends, and live well to be able to look after the child.

The single parent would be best advised, to keep aside the emotional baggage, past unfortunate events and distressing happenings, so as to focus on the present parenting needs and emotional security of the child. There should be no room for negative emotions like shame, guilt, anger, resentment, insecurity or blaming. The single parent, need to encourage and develop all the positive emotions like love, happiness, empathy, compassion and gratitude so as to strike a balance between work and home responsibilities. There is no need to prove to anyone, including self, that as a single parent one is a superman or a superwoman. The need is to learn to accept and acknowledge limitations and use strengths to the maximum.

Providing the child with love, disciplined freedom & space to grow emotionally and mature intellectually is the prime responsibility of the single parent. The child should always feel loved, wanted, secured at all times, and be permitted to form healthy relationship with peers. The child's mind need not be poisoned with bitterness, anger, hatred or cynicism about the other parent, or life in general, because of one's own insecurities and unresolved feelings. The child should be encouraged to take responsibilities for such things that he/ she is able to do independently, besides being involved in small household chores.

In the end, being a single parent may feel like a difficult journey to start with but acceptance, patience and emotional strength can turn it out to be a joyful adventure that could redefine his/ her life and that of the children.

Perhaps, in another 20 years or so, many successful people and community leaders of that period are expected to be from single-parent families. Going by such trends, we - as compassionate people with some wisdom - need to be concerned now, and look at if that generation children would grow up to be fully-functional individuals, or would they be vulnerable and emotionally less resilient?

What kind of parenting style would they be opting for, or what all life-options will they have to choose from, to finally arrive at decisions best suited to them under those prevailing circumstances?

Some thoughts to ponder upon!

<u>Stop blaming, to see problems with a different perspective</u>

How do most of us, generally react or respond when things go wrong? And, things can and will go wrong sometime or the other, despite us not wanting it that way.

When we feel a sense of shock, we usually say "how can this happen to *me*?" We find ourselves getting angry, and worked up. We immediately start to identify someone or something – may be a circumstance - to blame for the problem at hand. And continue working out a series of blames to fling at those, even before we have clearly established what exactly did happen.

This describes our typical response to difficulties we encounter, and we are not alone in this. Most people have this attitude. And, it is the easiest.

We all know, that there is no effect without a cause. We always look for the possible cause, behind what we experience. However, our search may not be always rational. When things happen the way that we don't like, our emotions get involved.

When we are emotionally aroused, it is hard for us to think clearly. Our "fight or flight" psychological response is activated. We see things in an all-or-nothing, black-and-white way, with no room for shades of grey. This makes us feel, very certain of our own view and perspective of things. We are then unable to acknowledge or admit any alternative explanations or possibilities. We feel "under attack", and hence are on the look-out for someone we want to call *"an enemy who has done this to me"*.

If we are <u>able</u> to find someone (and this is generally not so difficult) on whom we can put the blame for the problem being faced, it is very tempting to go right ahead and adopt this attitude without looking into the matter any further. The reason for this is that when we are frustrated, we feel some kind of "incompleteness" in our life, and all humans absolutely hate this. We all like to have things "made up well". We can feel immensely satisfied to blame someone, and give them a good bashing. That is another way of playing "a fool's game".

In our calmer moments, we can probably appreciate why the blame game is a fool's game. The hunt for scapegoats can distract us from reaching to the *real* root of a problem or difficulty being faced by us. We may somehow, find our scapegoat, but will totally miss the root cause. Which in turn means that, our unresolved problem is likely to return to haunt us - sooner or later.

Things can and will go wrong from time to time, no matter how careful we are. In such cases, looking for someone to blame is completely inappropriate. It also must be appreciated, that repeated instances of blaming can seriously and adversely affect our relationships within family, with colleagues, friends, and in our social circle. It is therefore very pertinent that we understand the need to stop blaming other people, and adopt a new different approach to problems.

The essential ingredient in adopting a new way to handle difficulties and disappointments is our "emotional control". To avoid blame seeking, we need a calm and dispassionate mind. If our emotions become aroused, we need to be able to calm down again and see the bigger picture. We need to begin, to make such a change by calling upon our inner resources. It may, at times, be difficult to easily "calm down" when we are indeed worked up, but is not impossible – in fact it is achievable. It is for the good of our own future life.

The quite often recommended exercises and techniques, that allow us to relax at a really deep level are one of the surest ways to achieve this. It gives us the space and flexibility to be able to see situations in several different ways easily, and to assume full control of our responses, and thereby the responsibility. We can learn to drop our blaming habit & behaviour. Replace it with a flexible attitude to go deep behind - and within - to ascertain the real cause of the problem. Talk it over, and discuss the disturbing concerns, rather than getting into an unending argument through our adamant approach. The first option leads us to positive results, while the latter to a situation where the suffering and aloofness begins.

There is a famous saying: A discussion is always better than an argument because an argument is to find out *who* is right, while discussion is to find out *what* is right.

This attitude will give us, new & different perspectives to face life's continuing challenges, and will stand us in good stead for the rest of our life.

Our fears, worry & anxiety – mindfulness frees us

All kinds of uncertainties are apparently growing not only in our daily life, but also all around us. Newspaper reports, environmental disasters and information overload assisted by technological advancements, are the main contributing factors as prime sources of our fears, worry and anxiety in life. We further add to this, our own unique and personal concerns – finances, well-being, education and life of our children, health of our parents as also ourselves – thereby making our life almost going out of control and balance on a frequent basis.

This directly leads to increasing discomfort, ill ease and loss of joy in routine living. Such kind of low-grade panic becomes our standard operating mode, and we then seek relief in work, food, drugs, sex, movies, television and even more work. All these things initially considered as relief, actually create more problems. Our stress-tolerating levels go down, depression sets in, and our fears, anxiety, worries & panic levels start increasing.

Fear in its most general form is defined as a feeling of agitation, apprehension, alarm or even terror caused by the presence of a danger or threat. It is one of the most basic of all human emotion and can be _felt_.

This feeling becomes *Anxiety* when the alarm or fear is not clearly or directly associated with any danger or threat. The agitation and distress is felt deeply in our mind as well as body. We are unable to identify the danger, but feel the fear anyway.

Worry, however, is the mind's expression of fear and can be seen as the combination of anxiety and similar thoughts.

Finally, when the feeling of fear is intense and sudden (though without any apparent cause) it is termed as *panic or phobia,* and it is usually so unpleasant that people even begin to modify and restrict their routine activities because of it.

The fear reaction is <u>physically</u> experienced throughout our body, mind and behaviour, because these are in a dynamic, continuously changing and interactive relationship all the time. Our heart pounds and pulse rate increases, our muscles tighten and a choking sensation is felt, we sweat or shake and numbness sets in, our breathing becomes difficult & abdominal discomfort is felt, and all kinds of body aches prevail.

Our <u>psychological</u> and emotional feelings get intense; we are unable to think clearly; we are confused with feelings of despair, restlessness, hopelessness and helplessness.

On <u>behavioural</u> front, we feel more irritable; our energy levels are low; we become more critical (of just about anything and everything); withdraw socially from people; undertake elaborate rituals and repetitive compulsions (washing hands or checking doors etc.).

We all experience anxiety and worries. It can be useful and helpful at times, so as to increase our attention - as required in the moment. Mild anxiety, can actually enhance our performance and productivity. When the fear, worry or anxiety reactions arise repeatedly and persist for long intervals, it is termed as "chronic".

This adversely affects our life towards relationships, work, social life and personal health. High levels of anxiety interfere with our daily life and normal functioning, and when it turns chronic it will need professional interference & treatment.

Towards a comprehensive treatment plan, some kind of self-help is a vital and supportive component, but not a substitute for the needed treatment. The self-help methods of mindfulness (present moment focus) have been recognised to play an important role in the treatment and recovery for individuals with anxiety disorders, and help them manage their fear, worry, anxiety and panic situations.

By practicing mindfulness, we learn to relax by cultivating "paying attention on purpose to this moment" in a non-judgmental way, so that so termed "problems" do not dominate our life, and we are in a position to offer more effective responses to them. Our inner strengths and virtues of compassion, kindness and gratitude help us transform ourselves to approach and accept the situation "as is", and face it, instead of running away from it.

Mindfulness helps us, to connect with each experience as it arises and flows through the present moment (like a passing cloud) when we make it a way of our living, instead of using it as a technique to be used only in rough times.

Mindfulness enables us to change - how we react or respond – in order to have a calm and relaxed attention to remain present and to be mindful. We can thus learn to monitor our thoughts and moods, learn to drop the disturbing ones and enjoy more joy as a result. This will lay a strong foundation for the presence of mind that is essentially needed to effectively manage our fear, anxiety, worry and panic.

Through mindfulness, we learn to become more responsive and far less reactive when fear, or worry, or anxiety, or panic does happen. The disappearance of *fear reaction* and the presence of *relaxation response* (when our heart-rate and breathing slows, blood pressure comes down, muscles soften, digestion improves, our thinking improves and we are able to concentrate) enables us to reverse the fight-or-flight activation.

We then have feelings of hopefulness and helpfulness, we are happier, we wish to socialise, our energy levels are high, and finally our body restores the lost balance to become calm and relaxed.

Loneliness – an insight

Some people feel like "it is heaven" to being alone and all by themselves - away from the constant demands of the kids, or a thoughtless/ nagging partner, or the hustle and bustle of work, or the hectic city life. However, and most of the times, when loneliness is prolonged, it becomes a haunting evil, slowly eating away at mind and life – leaving nothing but a sad and empty shell of a person with very little to live for. Those people then merely have an existence, with little meaning or purpose of life. But sooner or later reality takes over, and then they seek the company and closeness of another human being.

Loneliness may be a choice at times, but usually it occurs to people accidentally or because of unfortunate circumstances. The loss or death of a spouse, or a child, or a parent can lead to terrible loneliness. People can still live with other people in a house, be married and yet <u>in their mind</u> be totally isolated and feel lonely. They may have nothing in common with the person they live with, or they may be caring for an elderly helpless person who is sick, with a stroke for example, and who is unable to speak or respond. All this is part of loneliness.

All humans are social beings, and rely on each other not just for survival, but also for companionship, enjoyment and sharing pleasures in life. The "Hierarchy of Human Needs" model, developed by Abraham Maslow in the 1950's, identifies the most basic needs of people (food, clothing, shelter, water) at the bottom of a triangle, graduating upwards with more emotional and cognitive needs, and finally leading to the highest level or apex of individual human satisfaction called "Self- Actualisation". This model demonstrates, how and why individuals need basic support, understanding, education, intimacy, guidance and social support.

Loneliness is not necessarily always a negative and pathological feeling. It can some time, and to some extent, be just a part of normal person. For example, at times, loneliness may be necessary for reflecting on life and aiding emotional healing in any grieving process. It is not specific to any age group or gender, so anyone in the right (or wrong) circumstances can be affected. In duration terms, it can be short-term, or carry-on for many years.

Loneliness is a state of mind, and can still be present in a person despite being surrounded by many other people in his/ her life. People can feel isolated despite being socially active, or involved in sport, music, work, business etc. Men of all ages are more likely to suffer from loneliness, since they seek significantly lower levels of support and friendship, compared to women. Most men just rely on their wives or partners for social and emotional needs, while women generally have a broader social network, involvements and responsibilities for fulfilling their needs.

Severe loneliness and depression often seem to be natural partners - in extreme situations, it can even lead to suicide, if help is not provided, available or sought. Factors that can lead to such a situation include:

- ➢ unemployment and settlement issues at a new work place,
- ➢ financial hardship and extremely low self-esteem,
- ➢ droughts or floods that devastate lives and livelihoods,
- ➢ loss of partner or a loved one,
- ➢ unable or scared to make lasting relationships,
- ➢ stigmatic physical illness (HIV/ AIDS),
- ➢ problems of ageing (stroke, dementia),
- ➢ mental illnesses (suffering from phobias, anxiety and panic attacks),
- ➢ disabilities in which sufferers are discriminated against,
- ➢ highly stressful situations forcing people to move frequently from one place to another, without making friends etc.

The general symptoms of loneliness are wide spread, such as:

- ➢ feelings of loss, despair, isolation and helplessness,
- ➢ too much fear or anxiety and not being able to think straight,
- ➢ feeling down, worthless, angry, tired and irritable,
- ➢ finding it hard to sleep – not enough sleep and/ or sleeping too much/ little,
- ➢ being overly pessimistic or having a sense of failure or guilt,
- ➢ losing interest in other people and loss of outward affection,
- ➢ losing all interest in sex, and
- ➢ having negative thoughts which are unhelpful, involuntary and distorted.

To overcome loneliness, it is important to recognise and build our strengths and resources such as friends, relatives, skills, knowledge and so on, so that they can be harnessed especially in times of need – as also at all other times – to overcome feelings of doubt and negativity about oneself. The development of positivity can be achieved through love, compassion, gratitude, hopefulness, happiness, mindfulness and major decision to remain joyful.

Intimacy – issues and concerns

In our relationships, there are times when things are not smooth, issues arise that need to be addressed, and intimacy becomes flat and stale. This happens because people have conflicting expectations, get confused with other responsibilities/ issues, or have difficulty expressing their true mind. They say something, but mean another. The other person finds it equally difficulty in understanding correctly. When such conflicts arise between partners in relationship, intimacy is often the first thing that gets pushed aside, and sometimes they both just don't know what to do to make the relationship return to its original comfortable stage again.

The goal in an intimate relationship is, to feel connected in a deep and emotional way with our partner. A healthy intimate relationship should be having a sense of directness, as we experience being free to be who we are, rather than who we think we need to be for the other. Our intimacy needs to be safe, mutually supportive, respectful, non-punitive and peaceful – where we can feel taken care of, wanted, unconditionally accepted and loved "as we are". We experience forgiving and being forgiven, with minimum reminding of past mistakes, and find ourselves expressing gratitude for just being able to share our life with our partner.

People's feelings and the processes of relationship, should come before material gains and achievements. This type of relationship encourages our personal growth, supports our individuality and helps us and our partner becoming emotionally, physically and intellectually dependent on one another.

While searching for a connection of the heart and soul, many people think that sex is _the_ essential part of relationship. They even turn to sex enhancing drugs, as a way of trying to bring more intimacy into the relationship – the intimacy which is now missing or has evaporated over years of marriage or relationship. Intimacy is actually, not something that can be fixed with a drug. It takes two people – truly interested and willing – to work towards a deep spiritual and emotional connect.

In today's advanced world, we are no longer here for physical survival as our ancestors were, but more for a spiritual awakening. This awakening is happening in greater numbers now, because of people's desire to live more consciously and authentically in alignment with who they really are. Intimate relationships or spiritual partnerships, are helping people to do this.

Most of us spend our whole lives, consciously or unconsciously, trying to find our connection with _Spirit_. This is the same connection that we can feel in a deep union with another person. If there is distance between two people and they want an intimate connection, there is only one way – and that is to tackle, as best as they can, the core issues that they fear may destroy their relationship.

So, with that in mind, we should be aware about some basic issues surrounding intimacy – what is it, how do we lose it, and how do we get it back. It is not an easy task to define intimacy, because its meaning varies from relationship to relationship and even within relationships. In some relationships, intimacy becomes synonymous with sex, and feelings of intimacy may be confused with sexual feelings. In a wider view, intimacy has more to do with shared moments of closeness, or joy, than sexual interactions. But it is clear that irrespective of any specific definition given to it, intimacy and healthy relationships go hand in hand.

In true sense, intimacy is a basic ingredient in any meaningful relationship - which means being able to share all our thoughts, feelings and experiences. It involves being open, honest and vulnerable to another person, about our as also his/ her emotions.

Showing someone else how we feel, and what our hopes & dreams are, is a very important choice, and if it is with someone we love, it can be one of the most rewarding aspects of a relationship.

Forms of Intimacy & Improving it

As seen above, intimacy is a journey – it is not a tangible thing. It takes place over time, is ever changing, and never stagnant. In fact, any kind of stagnation in a relationship is bound to kill intimacy. Intimacy can also take many forms, and can be many things for different people... at different times.

One form of intimacy is <u>cognitive or intellectual</u> intimacy where two people exchange thoughts, share ideas, and enjoy similarities & differences between their opinions. If they can do this in an open and comfortable way, they can become quite intimate in an intellectual area.

A second form is <u>experiential intimacy</u>, where people get together to actively involve themselves with each other in mutually interested activities. This can range from a couple to a group of many people, and does not always involve talking or sharing, but may just include certain combined activities.

A third form is <u>emotional intimacy</u>, where two persons can comfortably share their deeper feelings with each other, or when they empathise with the feelings of the other person, really trying to understand other person's emotional needs.

A fourth form of is <u>sexual intimacy</u>. This is the stereotypical definition of intimacy, that most people are familiar with. This includes a broad range of sensuous activities, or expressions, and is much more than just simple sex.

As per research, few golden rules for developing, maintaining and improving intimacy in all relationships are categorised as – ABCDEFG:

> <u>Accept</u> personal responsibility: Blaming others for our own unhappiness is the number one cause of relationship problems – learning how to take loving care of ourselves is vital to a good relationship.

> <u>Be</u> open to learning: In any conflicting situation, we always have 2 choices: (1) we become open to learning & discover the deeper issues of the conflict, or (2) we try to win (at least not lose) through some form of controlling behaviour.
> It can be appreciated that, learning instead of controlling is a vital part of improving intimacy in any relationship. The subtle ways of trying to control others, so that they behave in a manner we want them to (e.g. anger, blame, judgment, withdrawal of love, explaining, teaching, defending, denying, etc.) do not promote healthy intimacy in any relationship. In fact, such behaviours create even more conflict.

> <u>Compassion</u> and understanding: When we desire to be treated lovingly – with kindness, compassion, understanding, and acceptance, why should we not treat others the same way?

➢ <u>Devote</u> specific times: Time is the essential part for successful relationships. It is vitally important to set aside specific times to be together, without which intimacy cannot be maintained properly.

➢ <u>Express</u> gratitude instead of complaints: Positive energy flows between two people when there is an "attitude of gratitude." We need to practice being grateful for what we have, rather than focusing on what we don't have. Complaints create heavy negative energy and stress, while gratitude creates inner peace that in turn affects not only intimacy and emotional health, but our physical health as well.

➢ <u>Fun</u>: We all know that "work without play makes Jack a dull boy." Same goes for dull relationships. Relationships thrive when people laugh together, play together, and when humour is a part of daily life. Intimacy flourishes when there is lightness of being, and not when everything is heavy.

➢ <u>Grateful</u> to the Almighty: For everything that we have, and by giving to other needy ones (whatever we have in excess) fills our soul and makes our heart sing. Doing social/ community services (e.g. at religious places) helps us move out of our own problems and supports a broader, more spiritual view of life.

If we all can practice these, it will be amazing to see the improvement in all our relationships, including our intimacy levels with our partners!

Fears – our friend or foe?

Ever since the beginning of civilization, fear has been a basic human emotion that has evolved primarily to protect us. It is that unpleasant sensation, which arises when we think we are in some danger – whether real or imaginary. It is also true, that behind every "fear" is a fear of losing something we value: loss of life, loss of health, loss of wealth, loss of well-being or loss of self-esteem etc.

Fear has two elements: a stimulus from the outside world, and our interpretation of that stimulus; and it is of two kinds – Real (or authentic fear) and Unreal fear.

Authentic or Real fear, is a primary human emotion and our important natural response to remain safe. It helps us, for survival in response to a danger in the present moment, and is the evolution's way to make our body ready for action - *fight or flight*. It is useful and makes us stronger to respond to the danger, while encouraging us to take immediate action to avoid that danger.

The Unreal fear, is stimulated by our imagination as to what *might happen* in the future, but has actually *not happened*. It is useful, only to a limited sense that we may plan and take some action to avoid the future danger. The worst things that unreal fear does is: to wipe out our critical thinking, cloud our judgment when we need to think clearly, and then our rationality to deal with the situation almost vanishes. That's why we need to learn to change our emotional state to feel better, irrespective of the situation.

However, the feeling of fear is always real, and its intentions are positive since there is always a value associated with our fear. We are afraid of a possible loss of something we already have, or is of some value to us. This value can be in terms of status, self-respect, safety, self-esteem or something we treasure – even the associated value from fear of failure or threat of rejection.

In the present fast-paced and achievement-oriented society, people do have anxieties about their performance and possible failures. And any kind of worry and anxiety, can lead us to have fear in the future. When these become intense, they can give feelings of panic attacks, or even phobia - which is just unreasonable fear.

Uncertainty of any kind is disturbing, and without proper information we try to fill the empty space with our imaginations, and that is what frightens us.

The only real fears that we all are born with are:

- ✓ fear of fall,
- ✓ fear of abandonment, and
- ✓ fear of sudden loud noises (thunders).

Real fear is natural and we *do not learn* it; while unreal fear *is learned*. Anything we were not born with, must have been learned by us while growing up, and can hence be unlearned.

We learn Unreal fears: by example (seeing adults), by experience (bad ones and pains), by repetition (consistent bad experiences and dealings) and by information (believing in dangers as from news stories, besides information overload).

The common fears as visible in adults are: fear of being alone, fear of heights and elevators, fear of social scrutiny, fear of flying, fear of blood, fear of doctors and dentists, fear of narrow confines, fear of open spaces, fear of failure, fear of authority, fear of animals/ spiders/ snakes etc., and fear of death.

Most of these unreal fears, are specific and thus have specific remedies. At times, the fear can even be enjoyable if we believe that the situation is safe & under control, there is no real danger, and the situation will end at a definite time (e.g. a ride on the high roller-coaster).

To quote, St. Augustine: *"The present has three dimensions – the present of past things, the present of present things and the present of future things".*

The cause of any unreal fear can come from – the past, the present and the future. The <u>fear from the past</u> leads a person to PTSD (post-traumatic stress disorder) – where the memory of a past traumatic event (abuse, torture, accident, unpleasant experience, war etc.) continues to trouble for many years. The past cannot be changed – we can only learn from it, instead of being fearful or afraid of it. The process of disassociation, helps in such situations to separate us from the actual event, and enables us to learn from that experience.

The unreal <u>fear about the future</u> comes from anxiety – what *might* happen? We need to change the way we think about the future, to stop feeling afraid right now and be able to *act* in the present, in a positive manner. We need to start thinking about what *we want to happen*, not what *we fear might happen*. We need to then plan some action, to make the desired outcome more likely, and then by taking appropriate action in the present, we can eliminate our unreal fears of the future.

We develop our inner fears when we are not in a position to control situations and surroundings. We are comfortable when we have more than enough resources to meet our challenges, but when we feel the challenge is greater than our resources, we feel anxious and afraid, and when it is considerably greater, we are even frightened. We need to learn to balance our resources & challenges.

Our family, friends and social circle are our resources, and they can provide the required support in situations when we are anxious or fearful. We need such people who believe in us, when our self-belief is under a cloud. They can hold out a helping hand and encourage us to make that extra effort, so that we can reach a little further than we thought we could.

To deal with our feelings of fear - both authentic and unreal - we need some ways to become more resourceful to take action. Amongst many techniques available to control the feeling of fear, slow and deep breathing is an important key as it helps to make us feel calm and relaxed. Another tool is by relaxing our body and mind, through some kind of meditation and mindfulness, to have complete control over our stress and anxiety. Simple relaxation exercises for a few minutes daily will make a big difference to our fear, and stress levels.

The first step needs to be taken – moving forward - so as to live a future life, that will be free from our unreal fears.

And, that step will make our future, now!

> *"Fear is that little darkroom where negatives are developed"* – Michael Prichard

Lessons from the school called "LIFE"

Let us try to draw a little comparison, between a small formal school that we normally go to during our childhood days, and the big informal school that we end up calling "Life" in our adult years. We are enrolled in both the schools, and we get the opportunity to learn our lessons, each day in these schools. We may like the lessons or hate them, but these are all part of our learning and there is no way out.

Human beings have, since generations, constantly endeavoured to discover the true meaning of life. In the course of this endless search, we all – as also our ancestors – have perhaps overlooked that there is no *one answer* for all. The meaning of life, is indeed different for every individual.

Each of us has our own goal, purpose and distinct path which is unique and different from others. As we travel our life path, we are presented with numerous lessons that we will need to learn in order to fulfil that purpose. The lessons that we experience, are specific to us – learning these lessons appropriately is the key to discovering and fulfilling the meaning & relevance of our own life.

Once our body has been able to teach us the basic lessons for survival, we are ready for the next teacher – our family – followed by the society we live in, and finally the ultimate teacher – the universal environment. We face, different opportunities and lessons in every circumstance that surfaces in our life.

When we experience pain, we learn a lesson; when we feel joy, we learn a different lesson; when we make a mistake, we learn another lesson. For every event, there is an accompanying lesson that must be learned. We would be lacking in our common sense, if we do not learn from all such experiences.

It is very much possible, that as we travel through our lifetime, we may encounter challenges and the resultant lessons that others may not have to face. Similarly, many others may have to spend their years struggling with challenges that we don't need to deal with. As an example, we may never know why we are blessed with a wonderful marriage, while our friends suffer through bitter arguments and painful divorces. As another example, we cannot be sure why we have to struggle financially while our peers enjoy a financially better life. Each of us, has to face and fight our own distinct and individual share of battles in life.

It can only be said, that we are presented with the lessons that we specifically need to learn, while others get their own set of challenges and lessons. Whether we choose to learn them or not is entirely up to us. The challenge, therefore, is to align ourselves with our own unique path by learning our individual lessons. This is one of the most difficult challenges we will face in our lifetime, as our path will lead us into a life that is radically different from others.

We may tend to compare, but we will not achieve anything by comparing our challenges with those around us. It will be a shear waste of time. We need to remember that we will only be faced with lessons that are relevant and specific to our own individual growth. And, others will have their own lessons relevant and specific to them for their individual growth. In simple terms, our destinies are different and hence the lessons to be learnt during the journey are different.

As part of the much larger mystery and perspective of "life", one of the important components is **"love"**. *We need to love what we do and do what we love.* We need to love our work, love our life, love our difficulties in order to learn from them, love our differences with others in order to feel distinct, and thus have a large store-house of inner energy with us - for various fulfilling activities, rather than be feeling pathetic over our adversities.

"Respect" is another component: when we respect other's feelings, emotions and position, we get respect in return. Love and respect, enable us to accept others as they are, and then to enjoy trust in our relationships because we will then accept even the differences, their weaknesses and faults - as much as others accept ours.

When we are able to rise to such challenges, we can unravel the mystery of purpose of our life, stop being a victim of fate or circumstances, and become empowered enough to be able to *create* our life, instead of just letting it *happen*.

When we decide to learn our lessons positively, we will be taking the first step in this direction to make our journey a useful one, to do better and to live happier. There is no end to improvement, and living life more purposefully & meaningfully. Such an approach will give us a new sense of freedom, new levels of energy, increased passion and a greater understanding of the role we and our beliefs play in determining the quality of our life.

In reality, it all comes down to a matter of choice. We can choose to be reactive and at the mercy of a threatening world, or we can choose to be responsive & open to life and its remarkably endless possibilities. We can be defensive and protective, or we can have a new spring in our steps and spirit, have eyes that truly see, ears that really hear, and a heart that can feel the wonders, and thereby celebrate the magnificent mystery called life.

We all can make a start now, since it is never too late to do anything. Belief and confidence in ourselves will create a magical power and ability within us to start on this difficult journey, to go through it, and complete it successfully.

<u>Dealing with</u>
<u>disappointments</u>

Many times in life, the result of our efforts is not as per our expectations; OR we face a totally different outcome from an almost predictable situation; OR many of our expectations out of a relationship are not fulfilled; OR we might not clear a prestigious test despite serious hard work; OR we might miss out on getting that plum position at work we always wanted; OR our best friend or family announces a move to another location; OR we lose a legal case despite being right; etc. All this causes disappointment.

Life is, and always will be, full of such disappointments. Many of these are actually out of our control. So, if we want to be happy and accept them on an "as is basis", we need to learn how to deal with them so that our disappointments could actually become gifts.

Disappointment, can be defined as the gap between our expectations and the resultant outcome. The larger is the gap, the stronger will be the disappointment. When things do not work out as we hoped or desired, the unfulfilled desires aggravate, which in turn fill us with negative thoughts and emotions. At such times, we may criticise ourselves saying that we are just not good enough, or that things never work out for us etc. We can become stuck with doubt, discouragement, despondency, despair, and depression.

Any disappointment is generally painful, and at such time it is important to be more specific and acknowledge what we are feeling? Maybe it is resentment, or anger at how we were treated, or a feeling of revenge toward someone who betrayed us, or blaming ourselves, someone else, or circumstances for what happened, or we are caught up in making excuses, or not taking responsibility.

Well, such reactions are normal after a disappointment, and have the power of holding us back. We need to identify the gap, between what "*happened*" and what *"should have happened"*, and thus have the clarity as to why we are disappointed.

Having done so, we then need to find out whether our expectations were fair and realistic, or did we see the situation narrowly? We need to ask ourselves "Do my expectations need to be adjusted for next time?" If necessary, we should not hesitate to seek a reality check from a trusted friend, because we need to essentially acknowledge how unrealistic our hopes were.

We all are far more capable of overcoming our feelings of disappointment, when we are able to re-connect with our overall purpose - by asking ourselves "why are we pursuing the goal in the first place, or how does it fit in with our vision of life?" This will give us the required courage and patience to stare down at the disappointment, and start afresh. We might just need a new way of approaching what seems to be the right thing. Our perseverance will allow us to achieve this.

Let us consider the example of the drawing, which from a closer point just looks like so many individual dots, and when we stand back at some distance, the "*hidden*" picture becomes apparent. Disappointment functions in the same way. It is not until we stand back, and dis-identify from our painful feelings, that we can see the big and real picture of the situation, including all the possibilities that are hidden within the disappointment. We then know, what we can learn from the situation, or what else we could do, or what could happen differently in future.

When we feel disempowered, we need to examine and identify our skills, inner strengths and support systems which will help us to turn the situation to our advantage. What additional knowledge do we now have that will make our future efforts successful? Amongst our examples in the starting para above, the lost court case gives valuable experience of how the justice system operates; the close friend shifting away gives the opportunity to utilise our own resources; a poor interview sharpens our skills of self-presentation for a job, etc.

Finally, moving through disappointment requires a re-appraisal of our objectives and expectations. To avoid future disappointment, we can ask ourselves how we may be able to pursue our objectives realistically, with less rigidity, more openness, and without losing hope. Maybe we can still keep the bar set at a high level, but approach it with smaller and more flexible steps. What definitely helps in the present, is genuine acceptance of what happened in the past, along with an equally strong commitment to move forward. Our wisdom and experience will give us the capacity to engage with the next battle, where we can win the war.

Increase Self Esteem, by practicing Forgiveness

Forgiveness is a very powerful and rare quality. When we forgive someone, we indirectly reveal something about our inner nature. When we don't forgive, we continue to hold onto our bad feelings and inner anguish against the person. The ability to forgive doesn't come easily to everybody, and when practiced, it sets us apart from others, and brings us respect.

Unforgiving people often feel that they are victims of other people's unacceptable behaviour. This victim mentality, can build up a list of things the other person has done & increase the resentment and anger inside us. Forgiveness releases these negative feelings, and helps people come together.

When a person views himself as a victim, he experiences pain. At times, it may be true that we have suffered at the hands of others, or feel that life has dealt us a blow, but even if there is a reason, we don't have to *feel like a victim* and pity ourselves – because we can rise above such events, and refuse to submit to them.

Bad things happen to everyone – that's just how life is. We can surely learn not to take each setback as a major event, and thereby avoid creating stress and pain for ourselves. What we tell ourselves affects our mood, behaviour and happiness. If we are negative, we cannot see reality and then our decisions are based on wrong assumptions/ interpretations. More bad decisions lead to more pain and failure, which will encourage us to believe that we are indeed a victim.

Negative comments from others, can cause us to further become more negative. A negative comment towards us may say a lot about the other person – maybe they have a big problem and that's why they are treating us badly. If we already have a negative mentality, we will just take what they say or do at its face value and believe again that we are a victim.

When we see ourselves as a victim, we feel that life has not treated us fairly. We become angry, and as a result start blaming everybody for our misfortune. Our self-esteem will be low and we will suffer from negative thinking of being trapped.

To overcome such victim-mentality, and to start building our self-esteem, we need to stop being angry or feeling helpless, question our negative thoughts, understand that we are responsible for our own life, and decide to do something positive.

We don't have to be a victim. Truly, the only person who can make us feel like one, is the same person who can free us from such a feeling – just ourselves!

We can achieve the following benefits, by being more forgiving:

- ✓ Our relationships will improve - to become stronger and longer lasting
- ✓ Others will forgive us more - when we act in a way that upsets them
- ✓ We will grow & mature as a person, and learn to handle our emotions better
- ✓ We will understand better - why other people act the way they do
- ✓ We will learn more about ourselves - what is important to us and what isn't
- ✓ We will gain tolerance of other's failings, and
- ✓ Our happiness quotient and self-esteem will increase many-fold.

Who should we forgive? Perhaps the simplest answer is - everyone!

We can be more forgiving:

- ✓ By recognizing our own faults – we will then be able to forgive other's faults
- ✓ By not placing such high standards on others
- ✓ By realizing that our values are different from other's
- ✓ By trying to see things from the other person's viewpoint as well
- ✓ By analysing what kind of a person are we? Are we perfect? Would we like others to forgive us when we make a mistake?
- ✓ By asking ourselves what we will gain or lose by <u>not forgiving</u> someone i.e. list the benefits and the negatives, (there will be many more negatives). Then make a list of what are the benefits and

negatives <u>of forgiving</u> that person, (we will actually see many more positives) ...

Soon, we will be able to understand, appreciate and practice the positives and benefits of forgiving.

Can we delay learning the art of forgiving, and improving our self-esteem? There is an obvious answer...

Anxiety

All of us have some experience, of how and what anxiety feels like – e.g. our heart beat increases before a big event, we get butterflies in our stomach at exam time, we worry and get upset over family problems, we are concerned about our performance and looks at special occasions, or we feel nervous at the time of asking the boss for a raise etc., etc. We are anxious just about anything. Actually, these are natural reactions related to our concerns about future.

It is a fact, that anxiety is an inevitable part of our life. There are many everyday situations, in which it is _appropriate and reasonable_ to react with some anxiety. In fact, if we don't feel any anxiety in response to some everyday challenges - involving potential loss or failure – it can be said that something is wrong with us. However, when it is _inappropriate and unreasonable_, it becomes a matter of concern, and that should be addressed appropriately.

It must be appreciated, that anxiety is different from fear or worry:

> <u>Fear</u> is usually, directed towards some concrete external object, or situation - such as not meeting a deadline, failing an exam, unable to pay regular bills, or being rejected by someone whom we want to have in our life, etc.

<u>Worry</u>ing can be somewhat helpful, when it prompts us to take action and address a problem. But if we are preoccupied with "what if's" and "worst-case scenarios", worry becomes a problem of its own.

On the other hand, focus of <u>anxiety</u> is more internal. It is our response to a vague, distant or unrecognised danger such as "losing control" of ourselves, or some situation, or a simple feeling that "something bad is going to happen".

Anxiety affects a person's whole being, since it is:

> Physiological: generating bodily reactions such as rapid heartbeat, muscle tension, uneasiness, dry mouth or sweating,
> Behavioural: adversely affects our ability to act, express ourselves or deal with situations, and
> Psychological: putting us in a state of apprehension and uneasiness.

Anxiety appears in different forms, and with different levels of intensity. Its range could be, from a mere twinge of uneasiness to a full-blown panic attack - marked by heart palpitations and disorientation, choking sensations, excessive sweating and trembling, nausea and dizziness, irrational fears, and having imaginary feelings of eminent doom.

Imaginary doubts and fears could be paralysing. They are least motivating or productive. They sap our emotional energy, send our anxiety levels soaring, and interfere with our day to day life - all without any positive outcome! The good and encouraging point is, that chronic worrying is just another mental *habit* – which we can also learn to break – like any other acquired habit.

An individual is largely responsible for how he/ she feels *What we say to ourselves*, in response to any particular situation, mainly determines our mood and feelings. This realisation is quite empowering, once we accept it as an important key to live a happier, more effective, meaningful and anxiety-free life.

Life need not be a *struggle* always – it could be *full & pleasurable*, with time for some fun, relaxation, and finally *an adventure*. Life can be converted from *helplessness to hopefulness* through Learned Optimism.

Who would not like to wake up every morning feeling completely calm and relaxed? We all crave for spending more quality time with our family, friends and loved ones, without our anxiety affecting our happiness. However, if anxiety is our major concern, we must remember that managing it is not a simple task - it is definitely a difficult inner journey that takes time, commitment and effort. Looking for any shortcuts, will only stray us from the path towards true self-management of anxiety.

Since it is impossible to be anxious and relaxed at the same time, strengthening our body's relaxation response is obviously a powerful worry-busting technique. There are many such techniques and strategies, we can integrate in our daily routine, to reduce our anxiety levels.

We can, with practice, train our brain to stay calm, relaxed and composed so as to look at life from a more positive, and wider perspective.

Anxiety Management Techniques

The capacity to relax is the very foundation of any program undertaken to overcome anxiety, phobias or panic attacks. Skills such as desensitization, visualization, and changing negative self-talk actually help us build our capacity to achieve deep relaxation through: abdominal breathing, progressive muscle relaxation, visualizing a peaceful scene, guided imagery, calming music, meditation, yoga and mindfulness.

There are also some things that we should remain away from, otherwise they will negatively interfere with our well-being. Taking coffee is one of the mistakes we all probably do, which we should stop because caffeine has anxiety-inducing components, and thus makes our anxiety worse. If we keep drinking several cups of coffee every day, while trying to manage our anxiety disorder, all our efforts will be severely affected. We can substitute it with a cup of hot chocolate, because chocolate has mild sedative effects, and when used in moderation, it will help us feel more relaxed throughout the day and keep our anxiety levels low.

We can try some of the following techniques, and can integrate our personal experiences to create our very own _personal anxiety management toolkit_, to be used in times of need:

1. Inhale Peace of Mind, Exhale Anxiety

Our breathing and emotions closely mirror one another. Anxiety, always makes our breath cycles shorter and shallower. Using our lungs, and inducing deep breaths will lessen our anxiety levels. Next time, when our anxiety is rising, we can use this simple technique. We can do it anywhere, and its effects are astonishing:

- ❖ Inhale slowly and deeply from the nose. Be gentle, don't force the air in.
- ❖ When the lungs are full, don't breathe out right away – take a small pause.
- ❖ As the lungs begin to struggle to release the air trapped inside, start releasing it slowly and steadily through the lips, making a slight sound.

Repeat these 3 steps, at least 10 times in a row. It would not take more than 5 minutes for this, and this much time will be worth its value. When it is over, we will feel much better and have a positive mood.

*Readers may please also refer to the 7/11
breathing recommendations under the "Calming
our anxious minds" write-up.*

2. Talk to Someone Friendly

When we are overtaken by anxiety, we are likely to lose our sense of perspective. Things will, perhaps always seem worse and magnified than they really are. This is easily addressable, by just finding someone we can freely talk to, and share our feelings, worries and troubling thoughts. A good and supportive friend can be extremely valuable, in helping us expel anxiety from our mind.

3. Engage in Some Physical Action

At the time of being anxious, our level of adrenaline is high, which makes our heart race faster, and we feel more tense and uptight. The best way to use that adrenaline is, by engaging in some physical exercise, or just get up and go for a long fast walk, or do some jogging, or play some outdoor game etc. These options reduce the adrenaline & help in normalising our breathing, and with a normalised breathing pattern our anxiety is bound to reduce. Doing regular physical exercises, therefore, is a must for people suffering from anxiety.

4. Learn to Relax the Body

Our inner mental tension also makes our whole body tight. We can reverse this process by relaxing our body, and our mind is sure to follow its lead. Here are some ideas we can use to achieve quick physical relaxation:

❖ Fill the bathtub and soak in for some time.
❖ Splash our body with cold water; then take a hot, steamy shower.
❖ Enjoy a good massage.
❖ Have a nap or just lie down for a while.

5. Learn to Trick Anxious Thinking

Our anxiety does not just come out of the blue. When we have anxiety attack, it is usually the result of a long-winded spiral of negative thoughts. Sometimes, we can keep anxiety at bay by closely watching our thoughts, and learning how to dismiss certain triggers that usually make us feel anxious. When we are worried about something, or notice some anxious thoughts creeping into our mind, we should try to confront those thoughts before they get too strong. This is the time to feed positivity in our mind and avert anxiety. We can ask questions such as:

- ❖ Is it true that I am blowing this worry/ fear out of proportion?
- ❖ This seems terrible now but will it still seem so a week/ month/ year later?
- ❖ Am I just making up reasons to keep feeling anxious and distressed?

We can think, make up, and form other similar questions – so as to disrupt our anxious-thinking mode. It will, enable our rational side to keep us away from getting caught up in the circle of anxiousness.

6. Listen to Some Favourite Music

There is music that soothes even the beast. Our anxiety is our inner beast, which can also be tamed. Try listening to different kinds of music, in various sound levels, at various places, to know what best soothes us. For some people, listening to classical music, or soothing natural sounds like running water or blowing wind does the trick. For others, singing along to their favourite singer or a song, is a sure-shot way to diminish their inner demons.

7. Find some Pleasant Distractions

As a general rule, all of us do not want to be distracted from our anxiety. Rather we want to hold it, and try to know its causes, so that we can smash them down into smaller, manageable bits. But, finding distractions is a much better way to avert anxiousness in those moments when we really need some peace of mind. Some recommended ideas are:

- ❖ to read a good book,
- ❖ watch an exciting movie on TV, and let the mind get absorbed in it,
- ❖ play some video games,
- ❖ paint a picture, or
- ❖ try doing some other activities of interest.

8. Embrace the Here and Now

There are numerous questions going on in our mind, including as to what is the source of all our tension and worrying at the moment. If we pause to consider these questions, we realise that we are feeling oppressed with just strange thoughts or terrible things that have not actually happened, and probably won't ever happen. Often, our mind is caught up in such negative cycles because we are not focused.

We should remember, that _worrying_ about a problem and _finding_ solutions to a problem are two entirely different things. We ought to make sure, that we are not wasting our energies "worrying", just for the sake of it. That's what most people do. Our ability to think is what makes the human race so special, but when we are always over-thinking about things, it turns into a bad habit. On such occasions, make sure to focus on what is around us: _the here and now_. This the only place and time, when we can really make the desired difference!

Readers may please also refer to few other "Mindfulness" related write-ups in this book.

To sum up: whenever we are getting engaged in negativity, our decision to counter it with positive, supportive statements - saying them loud to ourselves - will turn things around for the better. By cultivating the habit of countering each negative thought with a positive one, is one of the most significant steps we can take - in dealing with all kinds of anxiety, as also panic attacks. With practice and consistent efforts, we will be able to change both _the way we think_ and _the way we feel_ on a continuous basis.

By changing our thoughts, we will be able to change the way our world appears.

And, our world can be amazing – if only we **decide** it to be that way!

Overcoming Anxiety Disorders

Anxiety disorders are no. 1 mental health problem among women, and 2nd among men, after alcohol & drug abuse. In the recent past, nearly 25 percent of total world population has suffered from anxiety disorders, and is increasing in view of new uncertainties about: economic instability, performance competitiveness, relationship pressures, and other global issues like environment & terrorism.

We have mixed feelings about our worries – and those keep bothering us – we can't relax and get the pessimistic thoughts out of our head. Constant worrying takes a heavy toll on our life. It keeps us awake at night, and makes us tense & edgy during the day. Many times, we feel like a nervous wreck.

If our constant worries, fears, anxiety or panic attacks seem overwhelming and are preventing us from living our life the way we would like to, we may actually be suffering from an anxiety disorder.

An anxiety disorder is different from everyday normal anxiety, in a manner that *it is more intense*, and *lasts longer* (even after the stressful situation has passed).

Anxiety disorders are simply, an outcome of a reduced ability to cope with our stress – accumulated over time.

Human beings have always had to deal with stressful societal conditions, but the overall stress level is higher in today's hectic life schedule, than ever before. This is primarily on account of:

- ✓ Our social conditions have changed more in the last 30 years, than they did in the previous 300 years.
- ✓ Digital information technology has drastically changed our lives, in less than 20 years.
- ✓ The increased pace of modern society, has deprived people of adequate time to adjust to these changes.
- ✓ Cultural values, traditionally provided by society, are unclear.

All such conditions and uncertainties, leave a vacuum in which people are left to fend for themselves. The individuals then find it difficult, to find a sense of stability or consistency in their lives.

The symptoms of anxiety disorder often seem irrational and incomprehensible, while the causes vary not only as per the time period at which they operate, but also according to the levels at which they occur: Physical, Emotional, Behavioural, Mental, Interpersonal, Whole Self (Self Esteem), Existential, and Spiritual.

Some other causes are: heredity, childhood circumstances (parental support, emotional insecurity & dependence, suppressed expression of feelings), biological, recent stressors (short term, significant personal loss, life changes), conditioning (trauma, phobia, PTSD), anxious self-talk and personal belief system.

To address the varied causes and multi-levels at which anxiety disorders operate, the recovery also needs to be operating as a comprehensive multi-level approach - offering interventions to address various contributing causes.

Fortunately, there are many treatments and self-help strategies, that can help us reduce and control our anxiety symptoms, and to get back control of our life.

For most chronic worriers, the anxious thoughts are fuelled by the beliefs - negative as well as positive – that they hold about worrying. On the negative side, we may believe that our constant worrying

- ° is harmful or is going to drive us crazy,
- ° will affect our physical health, or
- ° we are going to lose all control over our life.

On the positive side, we may believe that our worrying

- ° helps us avoid bad things and prevents problems,
- ° prepares us for the worst, or
- ° leads to solutions.

Actually, while our negative beliefs add to our anxiety and keep the worry going, the positive beliefs about worrying can be just as damaging. In order to stop worry and anxiety for good, we must give up our belief that worrying serves any positive purpose.

Once we are able to realise that worrying is the problem, not the solution, we can regain control over our worried mind.

Tips for Managing Anxiety

When every day anxiety and worry dominate our thoughts, it becomes tough to be productive. When our anxious thoughts are uncontrollable, we may try lots of things: distract and tell ourselves to stop worrying, suppress anxious thoughts, reason with our worries, and try to think positive, but nothing seems to work for long. In fact, trying to do so often makes them stronger and more persistent, because it forces us to pay extra attention to the very thought that we want to avoid.

Tip 1: Create a worry period

To control our anxiety, we could try a different approach > rather than trying to stop or get rid of an anxious thought, we need to learn the art to postpone worrying i.e. to put off thinking about it until a later moment. The process to be adopted is:

a. **Create a "worry period."** Decide on a specific time and place for worrying. It should preferably be same every day (e.g. from 5:00 to 5:20 p.m. in the living room). We are allowed to worry about whatever is on our mind during this period, while rest of the day is a worry-free period.

b. **Postpone the worry**. If an anxious thought or worry comes during the day, make a brief mental note and postpone it to our worry period. We will have time to think about it later, and not right now.

c. **Refer to the "worry list" during the worry period**. Reflect on the worries noted during the day, and if the thoughts are still bothering us, we consider them. If the worries don't seem important any more, we can cut our worry period short and enjoy the rest of our day.

Postponing worrying is effective because it breaks our habit of dwelling on worries, without any struggle to suppress the thought or judge it. We simply *decide to do it later*. As we develop this ability, we will start to realise that we have more control over our worrying than we initially thought.

Tip 2: Is the problem solvable

Worrying and problem solving are two very different things. Problem solving involves evaluating a situation, coming up with concrete steps for dealing with it, and then implementing the action plan. Worrying, on the other hand, rarely leads to solutions. No matter how much time is spent dwelling on worst-case scenarios, we are no better prepared to deal with them – when they actually happen.

When a worry troubles us, we need to ask ourselves whether we can actually solve it all by ourselves. Productive, solvable worries are those we can take action on (e.g. worry about paying bills can be replaced by examining other flexible payment options). Unproductive, unsolvable worries are those for which there is no corresponding action (e.g. what if I get cancer someday or what if I meet with an accident?).

The following questions can help in such an evaluation:

- ° the problem we are having is true, or is it an imaginary what-if?
- ° If the problem is an imaginary what-if, then
  - how likely is it to actually happen?

  - can we do something about the problem or prepare for it, or

  - is it out of our control?

If the worry is solvable, we make a list of all possible solutions - without getting obsessed with a perfect solution; focus on the things we have the power to change, rather than on the circumstances or realities beyond our control; make a plan of action and start doing something about the problem.

But if the worry is not something we can solve, we need to learn to embrace and experience our feelings and emotions as a human being, without becoming overwhelmed, and in turn learn how to use them to our advantage.

Tip 3: Accept uncertainty

Most of us want to know with 100 % certainty what is going to happen in future. When we are unable to accept any uncertainty, doubt or unpredictability, it increases our anxieties and worries. Worrying is then considered as a way to possibly prevent unpleasant surprises, and control the outcome.

The hard truth is - it doesn't work. Thinking about all the things that could go wrong, doesn't make life any more predictable. We may feel safer when we are worrying, but it is just an illusion. Focusing on worst case scenarios will never keep bad things from happening. It will only keep us away from enjoying the good things we have in the present.

We need to examine the advantages and disadvantages of requiring certainty about everything in our life, the likelihood of positive or neutral outcomes, and whether only bad things happen just because they are uncertain. This will enable us to understand and appreciate the shortcomings of being intolerant and benefits of accepting uncertainty - to sail through our life.

Tip 4: Challenge our anxious thoughts

The people who suffer from chronic anxiety and worries may

- overestimate the possibility that things will turn out badly,
- jump to worst-case scenarios, or
- treat every negative thought as if it were a fact.

These irrational, pessimistic attitudes are not based on reality, and often are part of their negative thinking pattern. In order to break these bad thinking habits, and thereby stop the worry & anxiety they bring along, it is essential to retrain our brain.

We can start by identifying our frightening thoughts, and treat them as hypotheses under testing instead of viewing them as facts. As we examine and challenge our worries and fears, we will develop a more balanced perspective.

Further, we need to

- ° start looking at things in shades of grey also, instead of just black & white,
- ° avoid over-generalization and personalization,
- ° stop focusing on negatives, and develop positive attitude,
- ° completely stop jumping to conclusions, and
- ° start believing in ourselves.

Tip 5: Practice mindfulness

Worrying is usually focused on the future – on what might happen and what we will do about it. The practice of mindfulness can help us break free of our worries, by bringing our attention back to the present moment. This strategy is based on acknowledging our thoughts and then letting them go, like the wandering clouds.

We need to:

a. **Acknowledge and observe our anxious thoughts and feelings** – not try to ignore, fight, or control them.

b. **Let the worries go** - when we don't try to control our anxious thoughts, they soon pass, like moving clouds.

c. **Stay focused on the present** - pay attention to the rhythm of our breathing, and when we find ourselves stuck on a particular thought, to bring our attention back to the present moment.

Using mindfulness to stay focused on the present is a simple concept, but it takes a lot of practice to reap its benefits. At first, we will find that our mind keeps wandering, but that should not frustrate us. Each time we draw our focus back to the present, we are reinforcing a new mental habit that will help us break free of the spiral of negative worry.

Tip 6: Be aware of how others affect us

Our social circle greatly affects as to how we feel. Researches confirm that emotions are contagious, and we "catch" moods from other people - in fact even from strangers. So, the people we spend a lot of time with, have a greater impact on our mental state. We can therefore consider:

a. **Spending less time with people who make us anxious.** Start spending lesser time with persons who always seem to leave us feeling stressed or anxious. Instead, establish healthier relationship boundaries.

b. **Choosing our confidantes carefully.** Some people will help us gain correct perspective, while others will feed into our worries, doubts, and fears. Carefully choose whom to talk to when we feel anxious.

To summarise, all anxiousness can be defeated by accepting that it is there, understanding its causes, evaluating its solvability, challenging our thoughts, and learning to apply appropriate self-control/ meditation techniques as early as we can - to manage and deal with our inner turmoil, and to adopt best suited methods - commensurate with our strengths.

Readers may please also refer to "Anxiety Disorders" in another chapter of this book.

<u>Coping with Panic</u>

Can we imagine what it would feel like and how amazing our life would be without our anxiety/ panic holding us back? We can achieve such a life by understanding its probable causes, as a starting point. It provides us with a steady ground, from where we can build on our well-being. A solid house cannot be built from the roof down - it has to have strong roots/ foundation.

As we have read & understood (in some of the preceding chapters of this book), panic attack is a sudden surge of mounting physiological arousal that can occur "out of the blue". Its bodily symptoms are: heart palpitations, shortness of breath, choking sensations, dizziness and faintness, sweating and trembling etc.

These symptoms result in: feelings of uncertainty, a strong desire to run away from the situation, fear of dying, and/ or thinking that "the worst is going to happen". These are just natural bodily reactions that occur "out of context". Such a feeling is one of the most uncomfortable & frightening state of mind, which can have a traumatic impact on the sufferer.

The fact of the matter is, that panic attacks are more of an imagination of things "*likely to happen*", but have <u>not happened</u>. Since the related thoughts and feelings are more of an illusion, we can learn to cope with them to the extent that they will have no power to frighten us any longer. By making certain changes in our lifestyle, we can actually diminish their intensity and frequency to live a happy, fearless & satisfying life. The prime changes required to be implemented are:

➢ Regular practice of relaxation techniques (deep & abdominal breathing and mind/ body relaxation), and regular physical exercise,

➢ Elimination of stimulants such as caffeine, sugar and nicotine,

➢ Developing self-belief, which will promote within us a calmer and more accepting attitude towards life.

Once we are able to learn and implement these simple techniques, we can be certain that our panic related concerns will reduce to a large extent in an immediate time frame, and finally diminish over a period of time.

A few scientifically proven and researched facts & realities of panic attacks are:

➢ They are not dangerous or cannot cause heart failure or cardiac arrest.

➢ They cannot cause suffocation or stop our breathing.

➢ They cannot cause us to faint, lose our balance or control of ourselves.

➢ They cannot cause us to fall or cease to walk.

➢ They cannot cause us to go "mad or crazy".

We need not fight panic, since it is time limited, and will pass quickly if we do not fight against it, or react to it with even more fear. Studies indicate that when we resist it, it is likely to become worse. The following 4-step approach, has been found to be very useful and successful to take care of panic attacks:

- ✓ We should <u>face the symptoms</u> instead of running away from them. We need to convey to our imaginary thoughts, that we are ready to handle a particular situation one more time, as we have been successfully doing in the past.
- ✓ We should <u>accept</u> what is currently happening to our body (palpitations or dizziness etc.) instead of fighting it. We need to just observe and watch the physiological arousal of our body, without reacting to it with fear or anxiety.
- ✓ We should just <u>float with the wave</u> of panic attack, instead of forcing our way through it. We need to tell ourselves that, this is just a temporary bodily reaction to certain things and within a small time "this too shall pass".
- ✓ We should avoid saying scary things to ourselves, and instead give <u>positive affirmations</u> to our mind - treating feelings as just thoughts and not a reality.

Another point - instead of resting (as is recommended in a heart attack situation), we should physically move around, and actually do something which will use up our energy and the adrenaline created by the fight-or-flight reaction.

We can focus on the concrete objects in our immediate environment to ensure that we stay in the present i.e. now and here! Other simple actions, like unwrapping &

chewing a bubble-gum, counting backwards from 100 to 1, counting the number of people in the gathering etc., are excellent techniques to cope with the sudden attack. Engaging in something pleasurable, also helps us offset our anxiety and panic attack, since pleasure, anxiety and anger cannot be experienced at the same time. These are incompatible to each other.

Sibling Rivalry

The term "sibling" refers to children who are related by blood and growing up as a family. It is quite common, though strange, that whenever the word *sibling* comes up, the word *rivalry* seems sure to follow, despite the fact that there are many strong sibling relationships between brothers and sisters, who like and enjoy each other's company. Sibling rivalry has existed since times immemorial.

Rivalry is not necessarily a bad thing. It often refers to the relationship between competitors, as between two sports teams. Each team strives to be superior to the other, which is for the betterment of both. They play by rules of fairness, and tend to respect each other even as they try to defeat the other on the playing field.

The problem starts from choosing the word "rivalry", to describe the ongoing hostile relationship between siblings. Siblings don't choose the family they are born into. They don't choose each other. They share the one person, or the two people they most want for themselves: their parents.

The sibling bond is complicated, fluid, and influenced by many factors like position in the family, gender, age, and parental attitude. It often continues through the entire adulthood. While few adult siblings have severed their ties completely, approximately 33% describe their relationship as full of rivalry, or quite distance apart. They have little in common, and hardly spend any time together. Their old conflicts prevent them from seeing one another with a new or different perspective.

Parents' relationships with their children is also a contributory factor. From the age of one year onwards, children are acutely sensitive of how they are being treated in relation to their elder siblings. When parents are unable, or unwilling to monitor the goings-on between their children, inter-connections between siblings suffer.

Sibling relationships are not fixed, and they change dramatically over the years. Key life events in adolescent years, can bring siblings closer or split them apart. Similarly, life events in adulthood - leaving home, getting married, attending to an ill parent, grieving over a parent's death etc. - have the power to significantly improve the connection between siblings, or worsen & reinforce old rivalries.

As a matter of fact, siblings are such constants in our lives that they provide a reference point against which we can judge & measure our own selves. Friends & neighbours move away, former co-workers are forgotten, marriages break up, and parents die, but siblings remain siblings. As we age, and begin to feel our own mortality, many siblings re-discover the values & strengths of being together. Old rivalries are either forgotten or forgiven, and siblings concentrate on such feelings that can help them feel more connected.

When parents, who have two or more children, are asked a simple question "How do your kids get along with each other?", most often the answer is "They fight all the time, and have the <u>normal sibling rivalry</u>". The sibling rivalry, as such, seems to have been accepted as the normal state of affairs!

Parents generally become furious, when their child is tormented or bullied by other kids at school. But when it comes to their inability to make their own children stop troubling each other, they comfort themselves by telling that it is "normal." How acceptable can be the idea that bullying at home is normal, and even healthy, while school bullying is abnormal and devastatingly destructive?

This is because the word "normal" has more than one meaning or interpretation. A commonly accepted meaning of "normal" is "psychologically healthy," as in, "he is normal". Conversely, "abnormal" is used to mean someone who is "psychologically unhealthy".

Statistically speaking, sibling rivalry is indeed quite normal, because it is present in most families with two or more children. It is also considered a stubborn problem, because the harder parents try to get rid of it, the worse it tends to become. So, they get the impression that it is not only normal, but inevitable. Since sibling rivalry is commonly treated as normal, people also get the impression that it must be healthy, as implied by the meaning of normal (as stated in para above).

No, there is nothing healthy about the "normal" sibling rivalry. It is, no doubt, a dysfunctional relationship, that causes unnecessary pain not only to the children involved, but to the parents as well. The fact that most parents don't know how to stop or avoid it, does not make it healthy. There is little that grieves parents, when they see their own children - the people they love the most in the world - in a constant state of war. Ask any parent and observe the outcome.

Here are some do's and don'ts that may be helpful in reducing the sibling rivalry:

➢ Don't make comparisons: Each child is unique, and resents being evaluated in relation to someone else. Instead of comparison, each child in the family should be given his own level of expectation that relates only to him/ her.

➢ Don't dismiss or suppress children's angry feelings: it is certainly normal for siblings to get furious with one another. They also need to know that feelings of anger do not give them license to behave in cruel and dangerous ways.

➢ Try to avoid situations that promote violence in siblings: we must teach children that feelings and actions are not synonymous - it may be normal *to want to* hit the young baby, but parents *must not let any child do* it.

➢ Step in appropriately: siblings may want to settle their own differences, but it can be unfair in practice. Parents need to judge when it is appropriate to step in, mediate, provide guidance on how to handle conflicting situations.

➢ Talk openly: different children have abilities and talents in different areas. Talk openly about this

> reality with the children, so that they can begin to develop appropriate expectations for themselves.

➢ Acknowledge all behaviours: parents often ignore their children when they are playing nicely, and only pay attention when a problem arises. Behaviour modification tells us that, behaviours which are ignored go unrewarded & decrease, while behaviours which get attention are rewarded & increase.

Sibling rivalries can create certain stresses. But if overcome successfully, they will give the children resources that will serve them well, later in life. Siblings learn how to share, how to come face to face with jealousy, and how to accept their individual strengths & weaknesses. Best of all, as they watch the parents handle sibling rivalry with equanimity and fairness, they will gain that critical knowledge which will be valuable & helpful to them when they become parents.

Substance (Drugs) Abuse

Drug abuse affects people from all walks of life, irrespective of their socio-economic status. It wreaks havoc on the body and mind, and can eventually kill. When a person starts taking drugs, dependency on it can develop quickly, even before the user realizes that addiction is taking hold. When it becomes a full-blown addiction, it can be extremely difficult to stop the pattern of abuse.

In India, increase in drug abuse is reportedly growing at an alarming speed - needing immediate attention of health care professionals. Abuse of most substances, produces noticeable signs and symptoms – both at physical and behavioural levels. Learning to recognize such signs of drug abuse help prevent the problem from progressing.

Some of the noticeable <u>physical</u> symptoms of drug abuse affect the body's inner functioning. Changes in appearance can be additional clues to possible drug use and may include: bloodshot or glazed eyes, dilated or constricted pupils, abrupt weight changes, bruises, infections, or such other signs at the drug's intake point, disruption to normal brain functioning, and heart & organ dysfunction.

Drug abuse negatively affects a person's <u>behaviour</u> and habits, as he becomes more dependent on the drug. The drug itself can alter the brain's ability to focus, and form coherent thoughts. Changes in behaviour include: increased aggression and irritability, dramatic changes in attitude and social activities, lethargy and depression, and/ or involvement in a criminal activity.

Drug & alcohol abuse or misuse – excessive or inappropriate use of a substance – can be difficult to define. People's opinions, values, and beliefs vary significantly on the topic. For some, any use of an illegal drug or alcohol with the primary purpose of intoxication constitutes abuse. For others, abuse is indicated by recurring negative consequences, such as: failure to meet social/ work or academic obligations, physical injury or illness, drug-related legal problems, relationship problems with intimate partner/ friends/ family, diminished interest in normal activities, and short term memory loss or blackouts.

There are numerous reasons why people begin using drugs. Some start using it simply to see what the "drug high" is like. Drug use can quickly become "drug abuse", leading to chemical dependency on the drug and then the body doesn't function correctly without it. When the body becomes tolerant to or dependent on a drug, the user wants it more & more – to feel the same effects of that initial high.

Psychological, biological, social, and physiological factors might all play a role in whether or not a person reaches the stage of drugs abuse. A family history of substance abuse is, likely to make a person more vulnerable to addiction, besides other factors – such as peer pressure and ease of availability. Once a person starts using drugs heavily – increased amount of substance & frequency – physiological changes often take place and the person then becomes drug dependent/ addicted.

People may also feel psychologically dependent on a substance, particularly under stressful circumstances. Other signs of dependence are:

- ➢ Seeking the company of other users & cutting off social ties with non–users
- ➢ Dismissing or resenting expressions of concern from loved ones
- ➢ Experiencing withdrawal symptoms in the absence of the substance

Research indicates that the vast majority of people who are addicted to drugs or alcohol, mostly have some underlying mental health condition, or a significant psychological difficulty, or have their own not-so-happy personal experiences or memories which emotionally overwhelmed them sometime in the past.

Whether they are equipped with appropriate coping strategies or not, people who misuse substances rely on the immediate gratification of drugs as an alternative to facing the real issues at hand. But, in the long term, reliance on drugs and alcohol can only worsen any emotional or psychological condition.

The drug-user normally desires to avoid the very uncomfortable, and sometimes life-threatening, withdrawal symptoms that can occur when there is sudden discontinuity of the drug.

Breaking free from the hold of addiction often requires outside help. A person struggling from drug addiction does not have to battle the addiction alone. Drug de-addiction centres offer the support needed to beat the addiction, and regain control of one's life.

The first step to recovery, is ridding the body of the substance, and the safest way to do this is through a supervised detox program. While not all substances produce life-threatening withdrawal symptoms – as alcohol does - most others will indeed produce extremely uncomfortable symptoms, that are best managed under proper supervision. At the detox centre, the trained staff members and therapists monitor the process, and help patients get through it, as comfortably as possible.

A variety of addiction treatment centres, and therapeutic approaches exist to best match the specific needs of each affected individual, and specific programs give the person the tools he or she needs to live a happy and healthy life.

Smartphone addiction: While on the topic of addiction, it will not be out of place, to mention the most prevalent modern-day addiction of smartphones. It induces social and work-place problems besides isolation, anxiety, shorter attention spans, impulsivity, low self-esteem and instant gratification. It leads users to addictive behaviour, information overload, video gaming, and even pornography. The trend indicates that this technology addiction will grow, as technology advances.

Recent social networking apps like whatsapp, facebook, and linkdln etc. have further added fuel to the fire, and people from all age groups have already been adversely affected. The present trend of its excessive usage has started defeating the technological advantages that could have been ours.

Smartphone usage by youngsters needs to be seen to believe that addiction is setting-in pretty fast and deep. We can see them constantly checking their smartphones even when it does not ring, or getting paranoid when it is not with them, even for a short duration. Such a situation calls for professional help to break the cycle. The faster we can get rid of from all related nuisances, better it will be for all of us. Let us attempt to reap the benefits of technology to our best advantage, instead of getting negatively addicted.

Therapy to overcome addiction

Therapists who specialize in addiction recovery, often help addicted people to set achievable, and self-empowering short-term goals as they work to overcome their addiction. Once sobriety is achieved, adaptive skills can be developed as the person works to regain physical and emotional health. Then, they begin to employ new coping strategies in order to set long-term goals - that include rebuilding damaged relationships, accepting responsibility for actions, and releasing guilt.

Keeping in mind that the treatment is directed to the individual, rather than to the drug(s), the following principles aim to achieve and improve success, by ending (or moderating) drug use, lowering the risk of relapse, and allowing the persons with addiction to rebuild or restart their lives:

> Addiction is a multifaceted problem, but it can be treated effectively
> Treatment can be helpful, even if the client initially goes involuntarily
> Medications is an important part of treatment for drug abuse, or the mental health aspects underlying substance use

> ➤ Counselling and Behaviour therapies are highly effective, and utilized as the best available treatment options for drug abuse.

However, there is NO one approach that is appropriate for every affected person. There are different styles of therapy – Behavioural, CBT, and REBT - when attempting to find the right program for drug abuse counselling.

Behavioural Therapy is focused on obtaining goals directly related to the present life of the client, and works to examine behaviours that are unhealthy & undesirable, while identifying the situations that support their continuity.

In the case of substance use, the behaviour is likely to continue because of the role the substance plays in creating feelings of euphoria, calming the body, and eliminating pain. This creates reinforcement for the drug use to continue. Even when negative results occur because of the drug use, the person still values the benefit of its use, more than the risk of the consequence.

As part of behavioural therapy, **specific interventions** are used to address the unwanted behaviours including: education of the client on consequences and rewards, assertive communication, relaxation with tolerance, preparing individuals to explore, recognise & change their behaviour, and finally to accept treatment for their addictions, in order to get better and live a sober lifestyle.

Cognitive-Behavioural Therapy (CBT) uses behavioural therapies as a base, and assigns equal importance to the inter-connection of thoughts, feelings and behaviours. Negative thought patterns lead to unwanted feelings and behaviours, while problematic behaviours lead to unwanted feelings and negative thinking.

Here, the therapists try to understand the thoughts and feelings that <u>lead to the use</u>, as well as those that <u>occur following the use</u> of the substance. The therapist explores the client's flawed ways of thinking, that may sound rational at the time, while actually being irrational and illogical.

<u>Rational Emotive Behaviour Therapy (REBT)</u> is a therapy that has many similarities with CBT, but places less emphasis on the behaviours, and more on the <u>views and beliefs</u> (mostly faulty ones) of the individual. Using REBT, the client's faulty beliefs are identified and challenged. Once this is accomplished, new beliefs grounded in logic and reality, are introduced, emphasised upon and practiced.

The common **ABC model** of REBT works on the principle that it is <u>not the situation,</u> but the <u>belief about the situation</u> that creates the consequence. Normal saying would be that being offered the substance leads to its use, while REBT would say that being offered the substance **(A)**, leads to the belief that the substance would resolve a problem **(B)**, and this would result in its use **(C)**.

Multiple research has found, that substance use disorder is best treated through: mindfulness, **tolerance**, interpersonal communication, and emotional regulation - the act of identifying issues which trigger unwanted thoughts & feelings, and working to effectively reduce them through positive coping skills.

<u>Role of a Counsellor:</u> The prime role of a drug-abuse counsellor is to find the root cause of addiction, help patients progress into sobriety, educate them about its negative effects, and teach them to move-on through life without the substance.

A drug abuse counsellor initially helps to identify the addiction-related behaviour patterns, and then help confront behavioural and emotional issues that may be hindering the progress. Counsellors devote a great deal of time, energy and hope in their patients, and take pride on the successes of their patients.

Another key role of drug abuse counsellors is, to work with the families of patients as they move through the treatment. In addition to providing the addict with individualized care, counsellors will also educate the family on treatment, drug information, and the progress of their loved one.

A counsellors' job doesn't end when the patient leaves their office – they also help arrange additional mental health care & treatment that may be needed, through psychiatrists and psychologists. Counsellors are trained to think beyond the counselling sessions, and always make treatment decisions in the patient's best interest. Sometimes, the patient may be recommended for in-patient care at a substance abuse rehab centre, if that is considered best.

Is Marriage an Essential or Unnecessary Institution in modern society?

For centuries, our traditional society has treated marriage as an institution, and an undeniable establishment, considered to provide a good environment for a family. Marriage brings along a sense of responsibility that can help create & preserve relationships, and develop a strong bond between husband and wife. Secondly, married couples are more likely to create a good environment for their children – whose development stands to be benefitted by having both parents together.

Above all, marriage has been an institution, that has provided stability and cohesion in our society, and to thrive & progress since ages. The husband and wife together share and create a good soul-tie that permanently binds the two, even at spiritual level. The married persons also share money, property, other resources, character, habits, ideas, and such other essentials of society.

Marriage has remarkable and indelible effects and consequences on a person's life, and no human should take it lightly. And unwisely enter into it haphazardly, thoughtlessly, dispassionately, and without sensible, workable plan and purpose.

However, in today's liberal world, some people have started questioning the indispensability of marriage. Some have even gone to the extent of calling it an unnecessary continuance from the past – and feel that modern society can survive without it. In our contemporary world, when traditional values are shunned and new boundaries crossed, people are becoming more and more inclined to reject the idea of being with one partner for life.

The lack of understanding of the true meaning of marriage is a major cause for many broken relationships, marital separations and divorces, all around us. Such attitudes may lead to a total decline of our culture and civilisation.

In the context of India as a nation, the following principles could collectively form the primary reason for survival of the institution of marriage:

➢ Gaining knowledge about true nature, and acceptance of other people.
➢ Learning to build lasting companionship, and compassion towards others.
➢ The meaning and expression of true love, and affection for other humans.
➢ The right way to bring forth children, and establish true family life.
➢ Desired maturity in children, being nurtured and trained by both parents.
➢ The desire, willingness and courage to take up & accept responsibility.
➢ The transference of essential family values to other generations.

- ➤ Learning how to handle, effectively deal with, and resolve conflicts.
- ➤ Experiencing how life goes on in other families, as we merge with our spouse's family members, friends, and relatives.
- ➤ Rewards from children and other family members by way of care, concern, comfort, company, support, and assistance etc.
- ➤ Discovery of one's innate abilities, strengths, weaknesses and confidence.
- ➤ Enjoyment of a conscience-free, and satisfying sexual & romantic life.
- ➤ How we use the love and relationship with our spouse to challenge, break, make, teach, shape our character, and build godliness in ourselves.

It is recommended that we use this list to support and see if we really understand why we married (for married people); or why we wish to marry (for singles). Many more such points can always be added to the list above, based on specific circumstances, situations and needs.

Let us mull over these facts about America today: it has the highest rate of divorce in the Western world, increasing number of adults choose to live together without marrying, and more children than ever before are born outside of wedlock.

Many people are concluding, based on such studies, that marriage is not only broken, but also unnecessary in the modern world.

Dr.Keith Ablow, a psychiatrist, states in one of his articles that marriage is a dying institution:

> *"Well, I'm not certain marriage ever did suit most people who tried it. From what I hear from other psychiatrists and psychologists, and from what my patients, friends and relatives tell and show me through their behaviour, and from the fact that most marriages end either in divorce or acrimony, marriage is - as it has been for decades now - a source of real suffering for the vast majority of married people…. It's only a matter of time now. Marriage will fade away. We should be thinking about what might replace it…. We should come up with something that improves the quality of our lives and those of our children".*

At the same time, there are following observations, from other people:

> *"Marriage is not a dying institution, Commitment and Morality is".*

> *"We are becoming progressively more selfish, and marriage is not an institution that suits the selfish".*

> *"What's dying is the skill to maintain a long-term relationship. It requires actual work. And people either don't want to do the work, or they have no idea how to".*

"We have devalued relationship, loyalty and commitment in our society, and the only thing that matters is what feels good".

"While the marriages of our parents and grandparents had plenty of their own problems, families could count on the stability and loyalty that came with those relationships.... Not perfect, and not always functional, but the security was in knowing it would be there."

There is no doubt that marriage is facing some big challenges today, but it is difficult to believe that it is an outdated, or already a dead institution. I, as an individual, am convinced and believe that weakening of the marriage could be a disastrous trend – not only for individuals but also for our nation (India), and our culture.

With the above perspectives and observations, I leave it to the judicious and awakened mind of the reader, to draw his own interpretations and conclusion, on the criticality of marriage as a long-living, or dying institution!

Live In Relationships and its Impact on the Institution of Marriage in India

This is another much talked about, and debated issue in today's environment. India is a country where traditions, values, customs, culture, and beliefs are important parameters, as also sources of our daily life. Marriage here is considered a sacred union, a social institution, and also has legal approvals/ implications.

However, the western cultural idea of a live-in relationship, is gradually entering our lives in these modern and changing times. It is quite common these days, to see unmarried people staying together as partners. In such situations, various social, economic and legal issues have arisen and will continue to do so. It is under criticism, and is highly debated w.r.t. its legality and implication on our society.

The live-in relationship is, an arrangement in which an unmarried couple lives together in a long-term relationship - that resembles a marriage. In every day jargon, it is termed cohabitation. The relationship of a man with a woman in legal parlance is legitimate, if is based on proper marriage, and illegitimate if not as per specific/ applicable marriage laws.

Generally, the prime excuse offered by couples interested to have a live-in relationship is, that they want to test their compatibility for each other before going for some serious commitment. At times, the couples in live-in relationships also see no benefit, or value offered by the institution of marriage.

There is a direct impact of live-in relationships on marriage as an institution. The traditional Indian society, which has always regarded the institution of marriage as sacred, disapproves of such arrangements. The inter-dependence of partners on each other raises a question mark, given the instability of such a relationship. Even now, in many towns and cities, there is much social criticism, and stigma attached to such relationships. As a result, they largely remain secretive.

However, a huge societal change in the attitude towards live-in relationships can be seen around us. The concept of live-in relationships has come out of the closet, and it has even found partial recognition in law. The debate continues to rage on in public forums with various recommendations and opinions coming in to amend the existing laws.

Though there is no explicit legislation as yet, long term cohabitation between a man and a woman for a "reasonable period of time" has been equated to a valid marriage by many courts in India. The couple, thus shall be presumed to be leading a married life, and shall enjoy such rights. However, it is not defined as to how much time is "reasonable", to confer the marital status on such relationships.

Legally speaking, partners in a live-in relationship do not enjoy an automatic right of inheritance to the property of their partner. There is no specific law in place which deals with the division and protection of their individual or joint property, post separation. Bringing in suitable legislation, therefore, needs immediate attention of the lawmakers. In its absence, different couples may be subjected to different yardsticks when they seek their rights.

Another question arises: would that imply an extension of all rights of married partners to live-ins? This is rather earth shattering as it would destroy the "institution of a marriage".

Such decisions also contradict the law on bigamy. When bigamy is illegal for Hindus, it is unclear in what sense a live-in relationship can be equal to a marriage, if either the man or woman is already married to another living spouse. Personal laws differ for various communities in India on different matters, and to fit in live-ins into each of these would be a difficult and complex exercise.

However, with the increasing incidents of live-in relationships, "Reforms in the Criminal Justice System" 2003 report had even suggested an amendment of the word "wife" in the relevant section of law to include a woman who is "living in" with a man for a "reasonable period". Such an amendment will bring a uniform law, which would outline the rights, duties and responsibilities of such couples.

It is necessary to understand society with its changing colours, and provide laws which are practicable and enforceable to tackle these complex issues.

"With changing social norms of legitimacy in every society, including ours, what was illegitimate in the past may be legitimate today." - Justice A.K. Ganguly

<u>The Mirror</u>

I look in the mirror
And what do I see?
A strange looking person
That cannot be me.

For I am much younger
And not nearly so fat,
As that face in the mirror
I am looking at.

Oh, where are the mirrors
That I used to know,
Like the ones which were
Made thirty years ago

Now all things have changed
And I'm sure you'll agree,
Mirrors are not as good
As they used to be.

So never be concerned
If wrinkles appear,
For I have learned one thing
Which is very clear.

Should your complexion
Be less than perfection,
It is really the mirror
That needs correction.

(By Edmund Burke 1729-1797, Irish Philosopher)

<u>Choose to Live A Life</u>
<u>That Matters</u>

We all know it for sure that a day will come when our life will end – whether we are ready for it or not. We will not be alive to see another sunrise. All our worldly collections, treasures and wealth will remain here only, to be passed on to someone else in our family. Our physical existence will become irrelevant.

Our hopes, desires, aspirations and plans will be of no value. Even our grudges, complaints and frustrations will disappear. All those wins and losses that seemed so important to us will also vanish.

It would be of no significance whether we were good or bad looking, smart or dumb, brilliant or mediocre, or whether we were white or dark skinned, short or tall…

Still if someone would like to value the days we lived, it will be relevant to measure our life on some of these parameters:

- ✓ what we taught, instead of what we learnt;
- ✓ what we built, instead of what we bought;
- ✓ what we gave, instead of what we got;
- ✓ our contribution to the society, instead of our earnings;
- ✓ our character, instead of our enjoyments; and finally

✓ how many people will feel a lasting loss when we are no more, instead of how many people we knew.

Every act of our integrity, compassion and courage which could enrich, empower or encourage others to emulate our example will indeed matter.

It will be equally important and significant to know as to how long we will be remembered, by who all and for what actions of ours.

Living a life that actually matters does not happen by an accident.

It is not dictated by circumstances, but by choice. Our choice!

Can we choose to live a life that matters? The obvious answer is a big YES!!

Things that I have learnt

If you take the time to read these, I am sure you will come away with an enlightened perspective. The statements covered affect all of us, on a daily basis.

Enjoy reading...

I've learnt that:

- ➢ being kind is more important than being right.
- ➢ the best classroom in the world, is at the feet of an elderly person.
- ➢ having a child fall asleep in your arms, is one of the most peaceful feelings in the world.
- ➢ The child inside us should never be allowed to die.
- ➢ you should try to spend some time every day with someone who is less than 6 years, and above 60 years of age.
- ➢ I can always pray for someone when I don't have the strength to help him in some other way.
- ➢ don't walk ahead of me – I may not be able to follow you; don't walk behind me – I may not be able to lead you; walk besides me – and be my friend.
- ➢ when you tell me something, I will forget; when you teach me, I will remember; when you involve me, I will learn.

➤ no matter how serious your life requires you to be, everyone needs a friend with whom you can act foolish.

➤ sometimes all a person needs, is a hand to hold and a heart to understand.

➤ life is like a roll of toilet paper: the closer it gets to the end, the faster it goes.

➤ we should be glad God doesn't give us everything we ask for.

➤ money doesn't buy happiness.

➤ it's those small daily happenings that make life so spectacular.

➤ to ignore the facts does not change the facts.

➤ when you plan to get even with someone, you are only letting that person continue to hurt you.

➤ when you harbour bitterness, happiness will knock elsewhere.

➤ love and positivity, and not time alone, also heal wounds faster.

➤ no one is perfect, until you fall in love with them.

➤ under everyone's hard outer shell, is someone who wants to be appreciated and loved.

➤ the easiest way for me to grow as a person, is to surround myself with people smarter than I am.

➤ everyone you meet, deserves to be greeted with a smile.

➤ a smile is an inexpensive way to improve your looks.

➤ life is tough, but I'm tougher.

➤ opportunities are never lost; someone else will take the ones you miss.

➤ one should keep one's words both soft and tender, because tomorrow one may have to eat them.

> ➤ everyone wants to live on top of the mountain, but all the happiness and growth occurs while you're climbing it.
> ➤ the less time I have to work with, the more things I get done.

Good thoughts ought to be shared.

Go ahead and pass them on..

A wonderful life awaits ahead…